THE A-Z OF COMPANION PLANTING

by Jayne Neville

The A-Z of Companion Planting
Published by The Good Life Press Ltd. 2010

ISBN 978 1 904871 1828

A catalogue record for this book is available from the British Library.

Published by
The Good Life Press Ltd.
The Old Pigsties
Clifton Fields
Lytham Road
Preston
PR4 0XG

www.goodlifepress.co.uk
www.homefarmer.co.uk

Cover design by Rachel Gledhill
Cover Photographs © Stephen Studd
www.stephenstuddphotography.com

Printed in the UK by Scotprint

THE A-Z OF COMPANION PLANTING

by Jayne Neville

Contents

Introduction

Companion planting takes many forms. It can be used in practically any type of gardening situation and on both small or large scale ventures; for vegetable growing, in flower borders, herb beds; in fact, just about anywhere.

The basic idea behind it is refreshingly simple and straightforward – by growing in close proximity, certain plants bring benefits to others, resulting in increased yields and vigour. On the reverse side, there are just as many 'bad' companions as 'good' ones: some plants just don't get on at all - perhaps they give off a certain chemical which disagrees with their neighbour, or simply grow too tall or too vigorously, taking up most of the moisture or nutrients and leaving very little for the plant next door.

Companion planting can also take the form of a cover crop over the winter, preventing erosion of the soil and nutrient loss. Using the right companion plants rich in plant foods in this situation can also add fertility to the soil when they are cut and incorporated into the soil the following spring. This really is using companion planting to its best potential. When we delve a little deeper into the methods and the thinking behind companion planting later in this book, the myriad forms of this fascinating subject will be revealed and explained in more detail.

It is an excellent addition to the management of any organic garden. Growing things naturally is very satisfying and rewarding; in particular nurturing your own

Even something as simple as growing a tall plant alongside a smaller one can have positive or negative benefits depending on the varieties involved and whether they thrive in full sun or shade.

home-grown vegetables. As the saying goes, 'the proof of the pudding is in the eating', and what could be more true than producing your own crops for the table without resorting to manmade chemicals and other 'nasties' that harm our environment? Of course, the organic journey is not an easy one and without the aid of chemicals, can sometimes prove rather a challenge, but an exciting one – how to beat Mother Nature with Mother Nature! There are plenty of natural remedies and preventative measures to be found in the organic gardener's armoury – often you just need to know where to look.

Companion planting is one of the most useful and diverse tools in the gardener's arsenal. Ask someone what they think the term means and they are likely to say plants grown together that complement each other in a useful way. However, another aspect of companion planting is discovering that some plants don't get on, one or both having a negative effect on the other. Of course no completely natural methods can be guaranteed to always work 100% of the time, but anyone who has nurtured their treasured vegetables from seed, only to have them completely devastated by pests or diseases, will welcome all the help that natural planting schemes can give. Used on its own companion planting won't work miracles, but in a well cared-for garden the benefits will soon become obvious: reducing the numbers of insects, pests and weeds, providing weather protection and paving the way for bigger and better crops.

For many years now I have grown my own fruit and vegetables in a natural way; initially just for my own families' consumption then for a small vegetable box scheme I ran for several years. Over that time I must say that I came up against quite a few challenges and had to be quite flexible, not to say inventive, in my approach to protecting my plants from various pests and diseases. What made things more difficult for me was that I grew everything in the boxes, never relying on bought-in vegetables, so if even one crop failed, then my customers would miss out for a time on that variety until the next sowing was ready for harvest. This was something that had to be avoided if humanly possible! During my early gardening days – in a 6 x 8 foot greenhouse in a small town garden – whenever I grew tomatoes they were plagued with whitefly. I read that the strong scent of French marigolds apparently repelled whitefly, so tried my very first bit of companion planting with great results. Now I never grow indoor tomatoes without their protective 'friends' at their

side! This was a turning point for me and soon I was looking for more ways that plants can help other plants.
I figured that if people cared enough to buy locally grown organic food then they would probably be interested to hear what methods were used to grow it. Sure enough, the monthly newsletters I enclosed in the boxes were always welcome, especially when they included snippets on gardening lore and organic hints and tips relating to growing. Companion planting was one of the favourite topics and quite often I would include a sample companion plant alongside the vegetable or fruit it had helped to protect. Even if they didn't actually grow vegetables themselves, my customers liked to hear that something they were likely to have in their garden such as the little French marigold or the trailing nasturtium had played their part in protecting the very vegetables they were eating.

In the course of researching this book, I have come across many examples of companion planting being used, not just in domestic gardens, but in the gardens of stately homes, student plots at RHS Kew and even in a wildlife garden at Chester Zoo. Garden Organic, formerly the HDRA, use many companion planting combinations across their 10 acre site at Ryton near Coventry and they are well worth visiting to see companion planting in action.

For this book I have tried to gather together as much information on companion planting as I have been able – many pairings tried and tested by myself over the years, others from people I know and sources far and wide. Even so, the sheer scale of the discoveries made in the past and the possible combinations still waiting to be found mean these are just a starting point for your own companion planting schemes. Be open-minded, eagle-eyed and adventurous with your own plantings and you are very likely to discover even more effective companions yourself!

Jayne Neville,
Lincolnshire
March 2010

The History of
Companion Planting:
What Is it, Does it Work and How?

The pungent onion-like smell of chives can confuse and repel insects which otherwise might be tempted to eat your prized crops.

COMPANION PLANTING IS as old as the act of gardening itself. Both the Ancient Greeks and Romans have been noted for using it to benefit their plants. Observant gardeners down the years would certainly have noticed that some plants grew better together while others were quite the opposite and this knowledge has been passed down through the generations, sometimes lost, then being rediscovered again by someone else.

There is a well-known version of companion planting called The Three Sisters which was discovered and practised by native American Indians. This entailed growing sweetcorn, beans and squash in close proximity in the same field. Each plant supported the others in a different and beneficial way: the beans provided nitrogen for the nutrient hungry sweetcorn, the sweetcorn provided support for the climbing beans and the low-growing squash with its large leaves helped to suppress weeds and protect the soil from the effects of the weather.

Companions work in different ways. Some strong smelling plants repel or confuse insect pests, thus protecting the crops grown next to them, for example members of the allium family – onions and leeks – planted closely around carrots. The tiny carrot fly, such a major pest of carrots, finds it much harder to detect their scent when masked by the strongly scented onions and goes somewhere else to lay its eggs. For those lucky enough never to have experienced carrot root fly attack, it is the grubs that cause damage to the carrot roots by eating their way inside them. Whole sowings of carrots can be lost to this widespread pest and I have already mentioned the benefits of planting the pungent marigold close to vulnerable plants like tomatoes to prevent whitefly.

Strongly scented or colourful flowering plants are also useful for attracting beneficial insects to neighbouring plants. For example, the brightly coloured 'poached egg plant' (Limnanthes douglasii) that attracts hoverflies, a predator of aphids. Co-ordinated plantings in and around orchards of nectar rich plants will bring bees in to pollinate the fruit trees. The flowers acting as attractors will of course need to be flowering at the same time as the fruit tree blossom to have an effect on pollination. There are many strongly scented and colourful herbs which can be used in companion planting schemes, as well as providing flavoursome herbs for cooking. The pungent onion-like smell of chives can confuse and repel insects which otherwise might be tempted to eat your prized crops, and flowering thymes work in exactly the opposite way by attracting desirable and beneficial insects towards them.

Interplanting

Using plants between rows of crops to suppress weed growth is very effective.

Using plants between rows of crops to suppress weed growth is very effective, such as in the Three Sisters planting scheme mentioned earlier, where the squash leaves fill all available space, leaving none for any weeds. These will come up anywhere, particularly where

they are least wanted, so aim to cover all available space between rows of plants with useful companion plants to shade out the competitors. This is known as 'interplanting' or 'intercropping'.

Another technique to get the best use of available space and stop weeds taking hold is by 'sequential cropping'. This, as the name suggests, is planting crops in sequence, making sure that the ground is never left bare. For example, an early cropping variety is planted around a later maturing one, say lettuce planted next to squash or tomatoes. The salad leaves will cover the soil rapidly whilst the slower plants mature. By the time they are fully grown and filling the available space, the earlier crop will have been have been harvested and the weeds will not have been given a chance to take hold.

If you are growing acre upon acre of a single crop it is just like opening the door and saying "welcome" to all those creatures who would seek to eat it.

These methods allow a much more efficient use of space, particularly in a restricted area and careful planning will certainly result in your getting an extra crop, if not several, in the space available.

The success of companion planting lies in the fact that interplanting different varieties does away with the monoculture design of planting in the majority of conventionally laid out vegetable plots and flower gardens. By this I mean planted in straight rows or solid blocks where lots of the same plants are grown together as in rows of beans or blocks of tomatoes with nothing, apart from bare soil, in between. You might as well put a welcome sign out for all the pests – they will thank you for planting their favourite food in a convenient way so they can find them easily and move from one to another, feasting as they go!

Providing Physical Protection and Support

There are many plants that can offer physical protection to others from the elements. Tall windbreaks can be formed by plants like Jerusalem artichokes and sweetcorn to protect more delicate plants if there is no other available shelter in the garden. By siting climbing plants such as runner beans alongside sweetcorn, you can dispense with the need for bamboo canes as a means of support, as the sweetcorn will do this job for you. The sweetcorn stems will stand firm long after the cobs have been harvested so there will be plenty of time for the beans to produce their crop over the summer.

Taller plants that thrive in the sun can also protect small, shade tolerant plants. A good example is the tomato which needs sunlight in order for its fruit to ripen. An underplanting of lettuce will be shaded and so will be less likely to dry out and suffer sun-scorch.

In the ornamental flower garden too, plants can be used as supports. For example, growing clematis through a rose or even an annual climber such as morning glory or our friend the nasturtium could be trained through other shrubs to create a stunning display. Even better if each variety blooms at different times, providing a longer flowering season.

Tall windbreaks can be formed by plants like Jerusalem artichokes and sweetcorn to protect more delicate plants if there is no other available shelter in the garden.

Disease Control

Big expanses of plantings of the same variety are always vulnerable to the spread of disease and insect pest damage. These monocultures as seen in vast fields on farms are exactly what companion planting schemes seek to avoid; by their very diversity, plant diseases find it more difficult to establish and spread. This is why conventional farming has to rely so

Gardening on a much smaller scale often has its benefits. It is much easier to incorporate companion planting into a plan for home vegetable production and hand planting enables you to position plants more closely together. Weeding is never an enjoyable task, but it needs to be done on any vegetable plot. Little and often in the smaller garden is less odious than having to spend backbreaking hours on end weeding out those plants you do not want.

Trap Cropping

One companion plant can be positioned beside or around another because of its attractiveness to pests. This might seem strange, but these sacrificial plants are destined purely to become trap crops for insects to feed and/or lay their eggs on. An example of this is the brightly coloured nasturtium, with its fleshy, peppery leaves. If you have ever grown them in your garden, then you will know that aphids such as blackfly are very partial to them! This can be used to your advantage if you plant them nearby other plants they like such as broad beans – the aphids seem to prefer nasturtiums to beans. Another sacrificial plant is the fast-growing Chinese cabbage when planted next to a brassica crop. Once the pests have made their home on these trap crops, it is up to you what you wish to do. You may want to pull up the plants completely and destroy them or squash the insects on the plants if there are not too many.

much on chemical sprays to fight against an army of potential pests and diseases. Smaller quantities of the same plants are less likely to attract pests especially if they are interplanted with different species which are not at all attractive to the insects. If you are growing acre upon acre of a single crop it is just like opening the door and saying "welcome" to all those creatures who would seek to eat it. This applies not just to insects, but creatures such as rabbits and birds, which can devastate your plants. Once they know a good source of food is nearby and in vast quantities, your garden will quickly become their favourite restaurant! An often-quoted example of the disastrous effect of monoculture was the Irish potato famine in the mid 19th century, a classic example of how disease (in this case, blight) spread rapidly through a crop, rendering it useless and causing thousands of people to starve.

Soil Improvement

The most important nutrient for plant growth is nitrogen. The majority of this is in the atmosphere but of course for it to be of any use to plants, it needs to be in the soil! Members of the legume family (peas, beans, clover) fix atmospheric nitrogen for their own use and for the benefit of neighbouring plants via a symbiotic relationship with rhizohbia bacteria. Once these plants have finished cropping, they can be dug straight back into the soil. Nitrogen is stored in nodules on their stems and will be returned to the soil as the plant matter decomposes. Green manures, or plants grown simply for their benefit to the soil while they are growing or when they are dug into the soil are true companions, not just to other plants but to the soil itself. How to improve the soil in your garden by using green manures and other methods is covered in more detail in the following chapter.

Allelopathy

In simple terms, the term 'allelopathy' means the inhibition of growth in one species of plants by chemicals produced by another species.

The marigold's scent repels white and black fly, whilst the chemical released from its roots is a nematode repellent.

There have been very few scientific studies of companion planting, but this aspect really could be investigated further relating to this very unique chemical interaction between plants. It has long been known that certain plants do not grow well next to others and in fact, well before the term allelopathy was used, people observed the negative effects that one plant could have on another. Theophrastus, a Greek philosopher and botanist who lived around 300 B.C., noticed the inhibitory effects of pigweed on alfalfa. Later on in China around the first century A.D. Yang and Tang described 267 plants that had pes

The invasive ground elder can be halted by growing French marigolds amongst it.

ticidal abilities, including those with allelopathic effects. More recently a Swiss botanist, De Candolle, suggested in 1832 that crop plant exudates were responsible for an agricultural problem called soil sickness.

Some plants actually repel insects and once you know which ones they are, you can create a natural 'barrier' around certain plants prone to particular insect damage. The ways in which plants are able to do this varies; some exude chemicals from their roots or leaves and stems which can either repel or suppress some insect pests. Some plants can actually do both – the marigold's scent repels white and black fly, whilst the chemical released from its roots is a nematode repellent. The herb

Habitats

Useful insects need a suitable habitat in which to live, both in the growing season and over the winter. Aphid-eating lady-birds and other predators can over-winter in the hollow stems of herbaceous plants such as stinging nettles. Maybe this is a good excuse for not tidying the garden too much in the autumn! Mulches, old stacked log piles and fallen leaves are all potential winter homes for useful insects.

catnep, often referred to as catnip and, as its name suggests, a feline favourite, repels flea beetles – a major pest of radishes and other brassicas. If you have ever brushed against the leaves of catnep and caught a whiff of its pungent odour, you will perhaps understand why!

There are certain plants that definitely don't 'get along' if they are planted close together. Although most of the time this knowledge will help you identify those bad neighbours and plan your growing so that they can be sited well apart, there are odd occasions when one plant's negative effect on another can be a distinct advantage. Take, for example, that troublesome invader the ground elder. Anyone who has ever had this invasive weed in their garden will know that it is virtually impossible to eradicate once it is established. Spreading rapidly underground, digging out each and every piece of root is the only way of ridding yourself of it as it will regenerate from the tiniest piece. If it is growing under a hedge, then you're in trouble! Its growth can, however, be halted by growing French marigolds amongst it. Chemicals emitted from the marigold's roots are thought to inhibit the ground elder.

Useful pest predators such as ladybirds, hoverflies and lacewings are known to consume great quantities of aphids and feed on the nectar and pollen of plants with flat, open flowers such as the perennial cornflower, corn marigold, corn chamomile, ox-eye daisy and yarrow.

Contrary to popular belief, bumble bees are better pollinators than honey bees because they work more quickly, in worse weather and for longer hours.

Plants that Attract

Plants can attract both beneficial and unwanted insects into the garden. We have looked at plants that attract unwelcome insect guests away from the ones we want to protect, but if we want to increase pollinators or insects that feed on pests that eat our plants, then we need to know which plants are the most attractive to them.

In an orchard or any garden with a few fruit trees, it is a good idea to help nature along by attracting a few more pollinators (bees, hoverflies, etc.) than would perhaps be lured by the tree blossom alone. This is a field where experiments have been carried out (at the East Malling Research Centre in Kent). Useful pest predators such as hoverflies and lacewings are known to consume great quantities of aphids and certain wasps lay their eggs in caterpillars. These useful creatures feed on the nectar and pollen of plants with flat, open flowers such as the perennial cornflower, corn marigold, corn chamomile, ox-eye daisy and yarrow.

Many of the plants that attract pest predators also attract pollinators, as long as the flowers used to attract them bloom at the same time of the year as the fruit blossom we want pollinated. The orchard is of course a traditional

Flying pests are far less successful if their host plants are surrounded by other plants rather than bare soil.

setting for a beehive or two, and for several years we kept bees in our orchard. With a willow windbreak around the perimeter, both the fruit trees and the beehives were slightly more protected from extreme weather conditions. This was particularly useful in the spring when the trees were in blossom. Providing food for the insects prior to the trees flowering will also help build up young colonies of useful insects in the spring. This is especially true for bumble bees. Contrary to popular belief, bumble bees are better pollinators than honey bees because they work more quickly, in worse weather and for longer hours. Growing pussy willow along the edge of an orchard will provide food in spring for the bumble bee queens to get their first brood of the season off to a flying start – ready to pollinate even the earlier of fruit such as plums and pears. There is nothing like the gentle hum in an orchard as the bees and other pollinators go about their work in the spring.

Host-plant Finding Disruption

This rather confusing phrase simply refers to the use of companion plants to disrupt an insect from landing on and subsequently eating/laying eggs on a target plant that it finds attractive, eg. carrot root flies on carrots, blackfly on broad beans. Recent studies have shown that flying pests are far less successful if their host-plants are surrounded by other plants rather than bare soil. Basically, if there are too many 'wrong' plants in the vicinity of the target plants, and too many false landings on the part of the insect, it will eventually give up and go elsewhere.

An experiment with clover as a companion planting showed that 36% of cabbage root flies laid eggs beside cabbages growing in bare soil, compared to only 7% beside cabbages growing in clover. Needless to say, the cabbages grown on their own surrounded by bare earth failed to even reach maturity, with the ones growing with clover giving good yields.

Planting sunflowers with sweet-corn is said by some to increase the yield. If aphids are a pest in your garden then plant a few sun-flowers around. Then watch the ants herd the aphids onto them. The sunflowers are so tough that the aphids cause very little dam-age and the seed heads are an added bonus for the birds.

Plants that Support

Some plants can be of benefit to others by providing a support for the other to climb. Some companion plantings mimic nature by growing crop plants side by side with companions, so instead of having row after row of crops vulnerable to attack by pests, they are hidden or disguised by the leaves and aromas of other plants, like marigolds, borage and mint. The idea is that the presence of the companion actually helps the growth of your crop.

Sometimes the companion plant is not valuable in the kitchen, as with the wallflower or the daisy, but they still play their part in supporting their companions. Other times you might have two crop plants growing together, like carrot and onion or chive, the chives and onions of course, protecting the carrot from the carrot fly by disguising its smell with their scent.

Some of the many real benefits to be had from companion planting have not yet fully been explained by science, and include reduced attention from pests, increased growth and in some cases such as tomato and parsley, increased flavour.

The Push and Pull

Researchers at the Rothamstead Research Station came up with the concept of push and pull. Grow certain plants that release chemicals to deter pest insects and you create the push. Plants that divert pests away from your crops by attracting them to the companion make up the pull. The pull can also involve attracting beneficial insects too.

Plants that Push

Marigolds (Tagetes)

Marigolds give off an odour that insects can detect from hundreds of metres away and which acts as a strong repellent. Plant them very thickly throughout vegetable plots to keep the flying pests away. Marigolds also have roots that deter nematode (potato eelworm) attack, so planting them in the potato patch is a must.

Mints

Aphids and cabbage white butterflies hate the smell of mint. But be warned, mint roots spread like mad and soon take over the whole garden, so grow it in pots.

Rue

This plant deters weevils. Grow as a garden border or scatter rue leaf clippings in an infested area. Be careful: rue can cause rashes in some people, so make sure you wear gloves.

Sweet Basil

This herb is a must for any garden. Grow among vegetables to repel aphids, mites and mosquitoes. It is good in the greenhouse too, especially near peppers and tomatoes.

The Pull

Plants that have gone to seed are in the business of attracting all kinds of insects, and they can be used as trap plants. Chinese cabbages that have gone to seed seem to attract aphids away from other cabbages.

Borage

Borage attracts honeybees and so is beneficial for the setting of fruit. Mustard is possibly one of the best of the pull plants because its aroma attracts all kinds of insects. You can simply dig the mustard in like a green manure, covering it first with a layer of compost to stop the pest insects escaping.

Asters

Asters attract bees and spiders love them too. Angelica and morning glory provide a home for lacewings and ladybirds – both are excellent aphid hunters.

In a way, companion planting is garden ecology at work. The more we study our plots and get to know the likes and dislikes of the plants we grow, the better we will be at working out which plants do well, which insects are beneficial and which are simply pests.

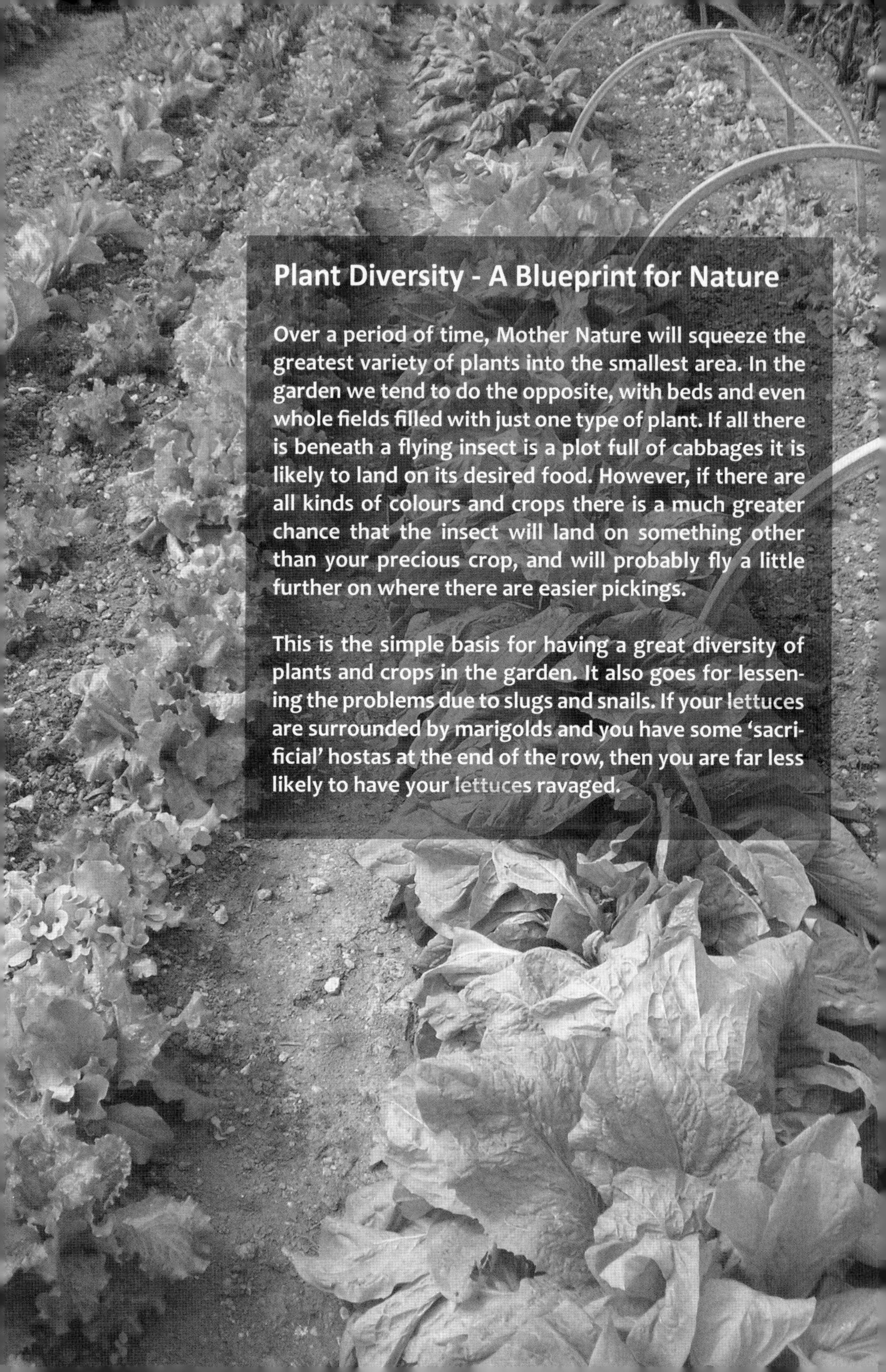

Plant Diversity - A Blueprint for Nature

Over a period of time, Mother Nature will squeeze the greatest variety of plants into the smallest area. In the garden we tend to do the opposite, with beds and even whole fields filled with just one type of plant. If all there is beneath a flying insect is a plot full of cabbages it is likely to land on its desired food. However, if there are all kinds of colours and crops there is a much greater chance that the insect will land on something other than your precious crop, and will probably fly a little further on where there are easier pickings.

This is the simple basis for having a great diversity of plants and crops in the garden. It also goes for lessening the problems due to slugs and snails. If your lettuces are surrounded by marigolds and you have some 'sacrificial' hostas at the end of the row, then you are far less likely to have your lettuces ravaged.

Square foot gardening is where the plants themselves create a protective environment by being packed in more closely together than normal, along with companion plants.

Some Good, Some Bad

There are many combinations of plants that are beneficial, but there are some that are really no good for each other at all. Garlic, for example, often taints the flavour of peas and beans and some cabbages. Onions have a negative effect on all kinds of beans and brassicas. Marigold roots kill off certain nematodes, and so plants such as carrots who suffer from nematode attack will do better when grown amongst them. The A-Z plant section of this book goes into more detail on various plants and their likes and dislikes, as does the companion planting table on pages 124 and 125.

Other planting schemes where you can use companion plants to good effect are square foot gardening (see above) and creating a forest garden.

A forest garden is where companion plants are intermingled with trees in a woodland setting.

Garlic often taints the flavour of peas and beans and some cabbages, so be careful where you plant the bulbs.

Getting the Best
from Companion Planting

ESSENTIALLY A TOTALLY organic method of growing, companion planting goes hand in hand with other natural ways of gardening. It is even more effective when the soil the plants are grown in has been enriched and improved by use of organic matter as all plants thrive in the best conditions, companions or otherwise. This chapter is all about making the most of what you have in your garden and how to improve on it using natural sources. Various ways of cultivating the soil, crop rotation, using green manures, composting and more are all covered here to help you make the most of your companion planting schemes.

Improving the Soil

Even if you start out with the very best soil, once you start using it for growing any sort of plant, you will need to replenish the nutrients they take out from it on a regular basis. Some vegetables in particular are very heavy feeders and take a lot out from

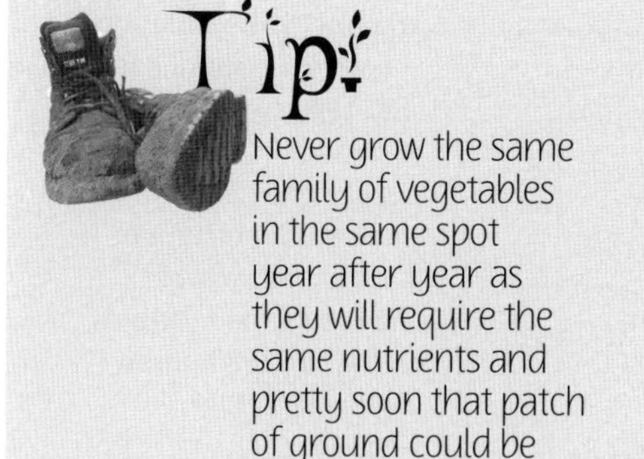

the soil – the nutrition you get from eating your own home grown produce will have come directly from the very soil your vegetables have come from, of course. This is one of the reasons it is important not to grow the same family of vegetables in the same spot year after year as they will require the same nutrients and pretty soon that patch of ground could become depleted or lacking in particular nutrients. This seasonal moving around of plant varieties is known as 'crop rotation' and will be covered in more detail later in this chapter.

Know your Soil

The starting point for any type of growing is getting your soil in the best possible condition. A good, fertile soil is the key to ensuring that crops grow fast and vigorously, which in turn helps them shrug off any threats from pests and diseases. If your soil is full of nutrients then your plants will produce bigger and better yields, and for longer. The structure of the soil too, plays an important part in the well-being of your plants. This affects moisture and nutrient retention and drainage. The bit of soil we are concerned with is the darker top surface layer (topsoil) which can be as deep as just a few centimetres, but hopefully more. This is the layer in which your plants will grow and is therefore the part to which improvements can be made if they are necessary. Under this is the subsoil, a lighter-looking, more solid layer, which is lacking in nutrients and drains badly. Fortunately, this layer is left undisturbed as plant roots rarely reach that far.

We will look at the different soil types and ways to improve them shortly, but if you are new to gardening, don't get yourself into a state just because your soil is too heavy, light or whatever. Most vegetables, herbs and fruit do get along pretty well in an average soil, most can tolerate varying degrees of fertility and there is also plenty you can do

Generally the thicker the layer of topsoil the better as this allows for roots to be contained in this (normally) nutrient rich layer, avoiding any contact with the much less fertile layer underneath.

to remedy the situation if your soil is lacking in any department.

Luckily enough for organic gardeners, there are several ways of increasing the nutrients in the soil and improving the structure.

Maybe you have heard the terms sand (light), silt (medium) and clay (heavy) applied to soil types? An ideal soil should be a nice even mixture of all three, but very few of us are so lucky to have just that and have to make the most of what we do have by making some improvements to it. To see what type of soil you have, simply squeeze a small quantity of it in your hand. A gritty texture indicates sandy, if it is sticky then it tends towards clay; a smoother and silkier texture means it is silty. Soils can quite often be a combination: for example, some clays can be slightly silty and some silts can carry more sand than others.

Soil in the garden is divided into three layers. The depth of each will most certainly vary from area to area, even from one part of the garden to another. The first layer, or topsoil, is the most important as this is where most plants will grow. Generally the thicker the layer of topsoil the better as this allows for roots to be contained in this (normally) nutrient rich layer, avoiding any contact with the much less fertile layer underneath. Even if the topsoil is lacking in nutrients or is shallow in depth, we can nevertheless make big improvements by adding lots of organic matter at regular intervals. Over a period of several years, a once shallow and impoverished topsoil can become rich, crumbly and fertile.

The second layer is known as subsoil and this is much lighter in colour than topsoil, being almost devoid of nutrients and containing no humus (organic matter). So you can see that the deeper we can make the topsoil, the less likely it is that plant roots will penetrate this barren layer.

Underneath all of this is the bedrock which is simply a natural rocky

Whatever type your soil is, it will benefit from an annual fix of organic matter dug into it. This improves the structure of a sandy soil by bulking it up and helping to retain moisture and nutrients more efficiently. A clay soil will be improved by adding grit along with organic matter which assists with drainage.

layer, usually buried so deep unless you live on the side of a steep hill, when the bedrock could be nearer the surface. Even on a slope with shallow soil, improvements can be made by adding lots of organic matter to raise the topsoil level.

The pH level of the soil is another factor which affects which plants will grow better in some soils than in others. If you're new to gardening then it is all too easy to become bogged down with too much information, so just think of the pH level as an indicator of whether your soil is acid or alkaline (limey). Most garden soils are somewhere in between and to find out what yours is, you can buy a simple soil testing kit from garden centres which will come with instructions and a result chart. Most vegetables grow best in a slightly acid soil with a pH around 6.5. The pH value of soil affects the way nutrients in the soil become available to the plants; in an extremely acid soil, calcium, phosphate, magnesium and potassium can disappear from the soil completely. Put simply, if your soil pH is drastically wrong then there will be no food available for the plants. Some diseases are more prevalent in certain soils too, for example, brassica clubroot can be more severe in acid conditions.

If your soil is around 6.5 (slightly acid) then it is as ideal as it can be for growing a wide range of plants and vegetables apart from a very few that need extremely acid or alkaline soils. Acid soils have a reading of below 7.0 and alkaline soils above 7.0. High alkalinity can be corrected by digging in plenty of organic matter, or if plants are already growing in alkaline soil, by using a spray containing seaweed to temporarily improve the conditions. You are more likely to discover that your soil is slightly more acid than it should be – this is quite common in the

UK, and this can be corrected by adding lime if the level is really acid. Only do this, however, if you really have to; if plants are growing well in it and there are plenty of earthworms, then it may be better to leave things as they are. Applying too much lime can also cause problems and it is better to use lighter dressings each year to improve the soil over time instead of one big hit which can be harmful.

What is Organic Matter?

In simple terms, this is any natural material that adds vital nutrients to the soil. An added bonus is that it will almost certainly improve the soil structure, allowing it to become most moisture and nutrient retentive, particularly if what you are working with tends to be one of the lighter types. Organic matter can be well-rotted animal manure, a green manure (plants grown in the soil specifically for cutting down and incorporating back into it to build up fertility), compost or even spent mushroom compost. Any of these are best dug into the soil over the autumn and winter months so as to be ready for your spring planting and sowing.

Any of these materials can also be applied as a thick layer on top of the soil and left for the earthworms to do their job and carry it down under the surface. Although this more natural method will take longer to get the organic matter incorporated into the soil, this thick layer, or mulch, has the advantage of acting as a weed suppressant through the year and will help the soil retain moisture in hot, dry weather. More about mulches in more detail later, however.

Where to Get your Organic Matter

If you keep livestock or know someone who does, then obtaining your supply of organic matter won't be a problem, but if you don't, getting hold of some can be difficult. Local riding stables are a good bet if you have any nearby and they may be more than happy to let you have a few sacks of horse muck.

Other livestock such as cattle, poultry and sheep produce manure that can be used to enrich the soil. Poultry manure tends to be very strong as it contains large amounts of ammonia but is great for adding to a

Of course, mixing fresh manure in with plant material in a compost bin is really the very best and cost effective way of getting your own nutrient packed compost.

compost heap amongst leafy ingredients as it helps break things down a lot quicker. (Neat urine does exactly the same job!).

Most horse or cattle manure will have been removed from stables or barns and will probably contain a reasonable proportion of straw or wood shavings that have lined the floor of the animals' shelter. In the case of straw, this decomposes fairly quickly and helps aerate the manure, making it break down much quicker. Many gardeners avoid manure mixed with wood shavings because it takes much longer to break down, and in fact you shouldn't add this to your soil until the shavings have disappeared completely as they use up nitrogen during the decomposition process, which is exactly the opposite to what you want. However, leave it for a year or so, occasionally forking it over to incorporate some air to assist the decomposition, and you will have something very valuable to add to your soil.

The quickest way to obtain manure to add to your soil is by buying it in pre-packed sacks from a garden centre, but this is a very expensive way to go about things! If you only require a small amount just for spreading around particular trees and plants to boost fertility then it does save hunting around for it and it will go much further. Poultry manure in the form of dried pellets can also be bought this way and can be sprinkled around growing plants or lightly dug in around them during the growing season as a crop-boosting quick release fertiliser.

If you have access to local manure - use it!

Making your own Compost

One of my smallholding heroes, John Seymour, author of 'The Complete Book of Self-Sufficiency ', once wrote 'Nothing should be wasted on the self-sufficient holding. The dustman should never have to call'. This sentiment is fundamental to any organic gardening situation, not just on smallholdings, because all organic matter from the house can be used to make excellent compost to improve your soil and feed your flowers, fruit and vegetables.

Any size garden has the space for a compost bin or container of some description that can be used for making lovely, nutrient rich compost. In fact, many councils these days positively encourage householders to do so by offering custom-made compost bins at reduced rates. Making your own compost is simple to do and apart from the initial outlay and/or effort involved buying or making the bin itself, it costs nothing and pretty much takes care of itself. You will of course need to add the ingredients in the first place, then turn the contents now and again to allow some air into the mixture. But by and large, that is pretty much it.

Making and using your own home-made compost is one of the cornerstones of organic gardening – it is totally sustainable and will cost you nothing but a little time and effort. Now what an incentive that is: growing the healthiest and best plants AND saving money... can you afford not to do it? Let's have a look at how it can be done.

Your finished compost will be rich, dark, crumbly and sweet-smelling and made up mainly of recycled garden and kitchen waste. Use it to feed and condition the soil and to make your own potting mixes. Around 40 per cent of the average dustbin contents are suitable for home-composting, so it helps cut down on landfill too.

If you're new to gardening, compost making can seem rather mysterious and maybe a little bit daunting, but all you need to do is provide the right ingredients and let nature do the rest. The following tips will help you to make better compost and more efficiently.

Where Do I Make my Compost?

There are a variety of compost bins on the market which you can use for processing your compost. A bin is not even 100% essential as you could simply build a heap and cover it over with some polythene or cardboard. For some people this is the only way they have ever made their compost. But if you want a tidy-looking composting area, bins do look neater and are easier to manage. Other alternatives are the traditional square ones made from wooden slats and these can be bought as kits from garden centres and gardening suppliers or you could even make your own. If you can get your hands on some wooden pallets you can make a bin from those, as I have by using four of them tied together, forming a square bin shape. The top is covered by an old piece of woven backed (not foam) carpet which keeps the contents protected from the elements and seals in the heat. Every now and then I turn the contents over with a fork to incorporate air which helps the decomposition process. When the compost is ready (this can take up to a year), all I have to do is untie the pallets, fill up the wheelbarrow and take it to wherever I need it.

What Can Go in my Compost Bin?

To get the best results use a mixture of different types of ingredient. The right balance is something you will learn as you go along, but a rough guide is to use equal amounts by volume of nitrogen rich and carbon rich ingredients (see below). You can also add smaller amounts of the items in the 'other ingredients' list.

Some things, like grass mowings, poultry manure and soft young weeds will rot down quickly. They work as 'activators', getting the composting started, but on their own will decay to a smelly and slimy mess.

Tough, 'woody' plant material is slower to rot but gives body to the finished compost – its bulky structure helps air to get into the compost heap and aid the decomposition process. Aim to make this the larger percentage of a compost heap. Tough woody items decay very slowly, so they are best chopped or shredded first to help them break down more quickly.

Compost Ingredients

Nitrogen Rich

Urine (yes indeed, this is one of the best compost activators!)
Comfrey leaves
Nettles
Grass cuttings
Raw fruit and vegetable peelings
Tea bags and leaves, coffee grounds
Young green weed growth, but avoid weeds with seeds
Soft green prunings
Animal manure from herbivores eg. from sheep, goats, cows and horses
Poultry manure and bedding

Carbon Rich

Cardboard eg. cereal packets, egg boxes, toilet roll tubes
Waste paper
Magazines and newspapers
Used pet bedding from vegetarian animals (rabbits, guinea pigs etc.)
such as hay, straw, shredded paper, wood shavings
Hedge clippings
Woody prunings
Old bedding plants
Bracken
Fallen leaves can also be composted or you can store them in a separate bin to make leaf mould to use as a mulch (see below).

Other Compostable Ingredients

Wood ash, hair, nail clippings, crushed egg shells, any natural fibres, for example wool or cotton

Do not compost meat, diseased plant material, perennial weeds, weed seeds, cooked food, cat litter, dog/cat poo (or any meat-eating animal's faeces) or coal ash (cinders).

How to Make your Compost

You can make compost simply by adding the above items to your heap or bin when they become available. Practically anything will compost eventually, but it may take a long time and if the mix is not balanced, will probably not produce a very pleasant result. With a little care you can improve things dramatically. You can even control the time it will take your compost to be ready to use. If you are in a hurry and need it available in a short time, and are able to put more effort into it, follow the 'hot' instructions. For the slower, less labour intensive and traditional method, the 'cool' method is the one to choose.

The Cool Method

If you can, collect enough compostable material to make a layer of at least 20cm in your compost bin. To start with, place several small twigs or woody prunings at the bottom to allow air circulation and drainage. Then mix in a selection of grass cuttings, soft weed growth, vegetable peelings, straw, woody prunings and screwed up cardboard packaging; all of it will help to create air spaces within the heap. Continue to add to the bin as and when you have more ingredients. If most of what you compost is kitchen waste, mix it with egg boxes, empty kitchen roll tubes and similar household paper and cardboard products to create a better combination.

When the container is full you can decide whether to just leave it to finish composting on its own, which could take up to a year, or use it to follow the hot heap method below.

The Hot Method

Collect up lots of suitable material to completely fill your compost container straight away. Some of this may have been stored in a cool heap and could have started to rot already. Make sure you have a mixture of soft and tough materials. Cut up or shred any tough items, mix everything together and then place it all in the compost bin. Add a little water and give the heap a good mix.

Within a few days the heap should be starting to feel warm to the touch. Leave it for a week or two to get going, then turn the heap with a fork. If you are making the compost in a purpose made bin, then remove everything from the container with the aim of mixing it all up. If the mixture feels dry, add some water to it, or if it is too wet add some more dry material. Put everything back into the compost bin.

The heap will heat up again because the fresh supply of air you have mixed in allows the fast acting aerobic microbes, ie. those that need oxygen, to continue with their work. You can empty the bin every now and then and follow the mixing process again if you like. Eventually, the heap will cool down and after a few weeks more will be ready to use. When the compost is crumbly, sweet smelling and there are no pockets of un-composted waste it is ready to use.

An Outdoor Compost Heap

A mixture of the two methods is probably best if you are going to make your compost in large quantities in a heap in your garden. It will certainly be almost impossible and incredibly hard work to completely empty the heap every time you want to mix it, so just turn the contents over with a garden fork when you have time. This will help it heat up. You can turn it as often or as little as you please, but the more often you turn the heap, the quicker your compost will be ready.

Depending on which method you use to make it, compost can be made in as little as six to eight weeks, or, more usually, it can take a year or more. In general, the more time and effort you put in, the quicker you will get your compost.

When the ingredients you have put in your container have turned into a dark brown, earthy smelling material, the composting process is complete. It can be left for a month or two to 'mature' before you use it.

Composting Bits and Bobs

Hedge Clippings and Prunings

Always chop or shred tough prunings and clippings from evergreen hedges before adding to a mixed compost heap. Compost large quantities separately; even unshredded they will compost eventually. Mix it with grass or other activating material; then water well. Tread down the heap, then cover it up. In anything from a few months to a few years you will have a coarse mulch which can be used on beds or borders.

Animal Manures

Horse and cattle manure mixed with straw composts well. Manure mixed with wood shavings should be left to rot until the shavings have decomposed before adding it to the heap as during its decomposition wood locks up nitrogen in the soil. Rotted manure makes an excellent mulch. Poultry manure is a highly effective compost activator, but needs to be used sparingly when fresh as its ammonia content is very high. Don't overlook the usefulness of manure from smaller pets like guinea pigs and rabbits either - however small the contribution, it can all go onto the compost heap!

A Leaf Mould Bin

If you have a lot of trees in your garden, then you will doubtless be busy in the autumn clearing up the fallen leaves. Well rotted leaves, or leaf mould, is a great soil enricher and to make your own is a very good way of using up all those leaves. A simple 'bin' can be made from four rustic fence posts driven into the ground to form a square shape. Fasten a length of chicken wire or wire netting to the outside of the posts with wire staples to make a bin. The leaves can be collected in here until the bin is full, then covered on top with a piece of carpet or thick polythene held in place by a couple of bricks. This keeps the rain off it. The leaves will take up to a year to decompose, but at the end of this you will be left with some very good material with which to mulch your plants or dig into the soil.

Here an enterprising council has left bags of leaves out for local gardener's to take advantage of.

Setting up a Wormery

Another excellent way of making super-rich compost, albeit in smaller amounts, is by setting up a worm bin or wormery. Wormeries are great because you can add most of your household waste to them and the worms will turn it into luscious, nutritious compost.

Basically, a wormery is a container housing a colony of special types of worms, known as brandling or tiger worms. Worm bins can be kept indoors or out and are ideal for households with no garden as they produce only a small quantity of compost and a liquid which can be used as a concentrated plant food. There are a variety of worm bins available for sale, complete with "worm starter kits". However, it is possible to make your own and suitable worms for making worm compost can be bought from fishing shops. The one I have myself is made from a tall heavy duty plastic wheelie-type bin with a hinged lid and ventilation holes, but here is all you need to know about making your very own.

What you Will Need...

Around 400 compost worms (often called tiger or brandling worms). These are available from fishing tackle shops or via mail order (see the supplier section at the back of this book).

A plastic dustbin with lid / a plastic tap / some sand or gravel / a few small pieces of wood / a small quantity of bedding material.

And Here's How to Make it...

Drill some air holes into the lid of the bin so the worms can breathe and the bin is ventilated.

Place 3-4 inches of sand or gravel at the bottom of the bin for drainage.

Place wooden slats on top of the sand or gravel, to separate the drainage material from the compost you are going to produce.

On top of the wooden slats, put down 4 inches of damp bedding material. Shredded newspaper or straw makes ideal bedding for wormeries.

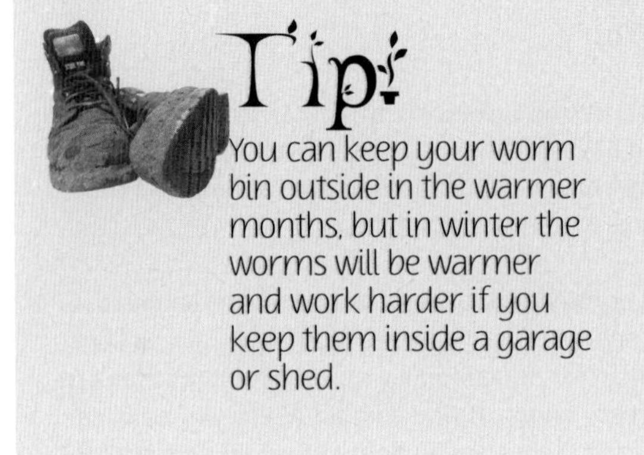

Drill a tap into the bin just above the gravel / sand, slightly above where the wooden slats are situated. Taps can be obtained from hard-ware / DIY shops.

Once your wormery is complete, make an indentation in the bedding material and place the worms inside it. Once you have done that you can start adding your food scraps. Always make sure the scraps are chopped up well. There are two main ways of feeding the worms:

Place the food scraps on the surface of the bedding in a layer (up to 2" deep), but never cover the whole surface as the worms need a small area to escape if conditions get unpleasant.

Alternatively you can bury small batches of food scraps in the bedding, around the bin. Some people prefer this way as they feel the waste is covered up and is out of the way of the flies.

With both methods you need to keep a thick sheet of wet newspapers over the surface to keep the light out and moisture in. Only add more food when the worms have finished or practically finished their meal. The speed the food is processed will depend on the number of worms, the time of year and the type of food added. Never overfeed your wor-mery. Keep a check to see that the things you put in it are being eaten by the worms, otherwise the food will just rot, and the bin will begin to smell nasty. The worms won't find it too pleasant, either!

After a few weeks you should be able to collect some liquid through the tap which you can use as a liquid feed for your plants. After a few months the worms should have made you a useful amount of compost, which you can remove from the bin and use wherever you want. Don't forget to carefully sort out the worms so you can put them back in the wormery and start again.

CONTENTS OF YOUR WORM COMPOST BIN	
Do put in	Don't put in
Fruit and vegetable leftovers and peelings (chopped up before adding)	Meat and fish (will smell unpleasant as they rot and possibly attract vermin and flies)
Egg shells (will provide calcium for the worms and combat acidity in the wormery)	Diseased plants
Green leaves, tea leaves and coffee grounds, annual weeds (without seed heads)	Large quantities of grass cuttings (this can heat up, ferment and give off ammonia, which can be fatal for worms)
Cow and / or horse manure	Annual weeds with seeds on (OK if leaves and stems only), cheese and other processed products, dog / cat faeces, cooked food eg. baked beans, potatoes)
Cereals, bread	

No-dig cultivation

An alternative way of managing soil is known as 'no dig' cultivation. The no-dig garden is usually divided into beds, which makes them easy to reach from each side. They are prepared by an initial double digging and incorporating a quantity of bulky organic matter. The soil is later worked down to a fine tilth. Once they have been dug the beds are not walked on, which helps avoid compacting the soil. The beds are also covered as much as possible by crops, green manures and mulches to avoid damage from heavy rain and to minimize nutrient loss.

In no-dig gardens organic matter and manures are applied as surface mulches in the autumn or while crops are growing if extra nutrients are required by heavy feeders. This works well on clay soils but on very light soils it might not be possible to incorporate enough material without cultivation. The answer, in this instance, is to incorporate manure into the top few inches with minimum soil disturbance.

There are other very good reasons to limit the disturbance of top soil. Over recent years research has been carried out into the bacteria and fungi that live in soil. We all know that there are some nasty fungi around, things like clubroot are rife on many allotments, but there are also many beneficial fungi that work with plants. Beneficial fungi live by attaching themselves to the roots of plants. The surface area of the fungus is very much greater than the area of the roots so the fungi effectively extend the feeding area of the plant. They work in harmony with the plant by helping it to absorb more water and nutrients, in return the plant provides food for the fungus. Having useful things in the soil is of obvious benefit, but they are delicate and prefer soil that is not disturbed, so they tend to thrive in 'no dig' gardens with a high organic content. Another major benefit of not digging is the decrease in the number of weeds. Every time you turn over soil more weed seeds are exposed to light and can germinate. Over time, no-dig beds have fewer and fewer weeds until eventually there are hardly any at all.

Using the no-dig method of gardening provides some interesting ways of growing crops: potatoes cannot be earthed up in the usual way but are grown on the surface and covered with a straw or other mulch. This makes it very easy to harvest the crop as all that is required is to remove some of the mulch, pick up the quantity of potatoes required and replace the mulch.

The No-dig Technique

Bizarrely, the initial preparation of your 'no-dig' beds will require some pretty strenuous digging, but of course you are only ever going to have to do this once, so it will be worth the effort!

Double dig your beds, making them around 4ft (1.1m) wide. To double dig, firstly dig a wide trench about 40cm / 16inches wide. The soil you remove needs to be transported down to the other end of the bed by wheelbarrow to fill the final trench you dig. Fork over the soil in the first trench fairly deeply then add plenty of well-rotted animal manure. Mix this together with soil from the next trench in line, which will fill the first trench, leaving the following one ready for adding the next batch of manure. Keep working along, trench by trench, until you reach the last one. The soil in your barrow will go in the very last trench.

You can edge the beds with timber if required, but try to avoid using pressure treated wood as there is a possibility that the chemicals used to preserve it can leach into the soil.

Avoid walking on the soil again, even using boards.

Keep the soil covered as much as possible to protect it from heavy rain which causes compaction.

In winter use green manures, mulches or garden compost covered by black plastic to protect the bed from the worst of the weather.

Make paths around the beds at least 2ft (60cms) wide. They can be covered with a permeable membrane, chopped bark or any other weed suppressor.

Making your own Liquid Fertilisers

Some plants truly become 'good companions' when they are transformed into liquid fertiliser.

In the A-Z section of this book I extol the virtues of stinging nettles and comfrey as perfect ingredients for making effective liquid fertilisers. Both these plants, along with animal manure, can be used for making a nutrient boosting soil improver which is simple to make, costs nothing and is, above all, natural.

Most plants will appreciate a dose of a liquid feed packed with nitrogen, phosphate and potash now and again in the growing season as a general purpose fertiliser, but for heavy cropping vegetables such as tomatoes, aubergines and peppers it is almost essential if you want exceptional yields.

I make all my liquid feeds in an old plastic water butt with a tap at the bottom. The butt stands on bricks to raise it off the ground and make access to the tap easier. It is placed a long way from the house because, as you will soon find out, the resulting liquid is rather pungent! For this reason, and to keep the flies at bay, the butt also needs a snug fitting lid.

If you don't want or need huge quantities of either, but still would like to try making your own, then a covered bucket will do – half filled with leaves then topped up to the brim with water. You will know when it is ready because you will smell it – just don't inhale too deeply!

You can make a concentrated liquid which will need diluting x 15 with water by packing the bottom of the butt with a very thick layer of comfrey leaves. You will need to apply weight on top of it to compress the leaves in order to extract comfrey liquid over the next few weeks. A plywood board weighted down with two or three bricks should do the trick. Keep the tap open with a glass jam jar underneath to catch the liquid. A quicker method is to fill the butt about a quarter full of water then add fresh comfrey leaves to it and give it all a stir. Replace the lid of the butt and after a couple of weeks the leaves will have started to decompose and dissolve, resulting in a ready-diluted mixture to use on your vegetables.

You can make a very similar liquid feed using stinging nettles. The best time to make it is early in the year when the plants will have plenty of young, tender leaves which will break down quickly. You can use either of the methods above to make a concentrated or ready-diluted nettle feed.

If you don't want or need huge quantities of either, but still would like to try making your own, then a covered bucket will do – half filled with leaves then topped up to the brim with water. You will know when it is ready because you will smell it – just don't inhale too deeply!

Natural Mulches

Mulching (using comfrey, nettles and fallen leaves) the surface of the soil has a multitude of benefits in an organic garden and it is very easy to do. You can buy purpose made products such as woven mulch sheets, sacks of forest bark or even use old carpets to spread around plants, but there are much more environmentally friendly and cheaper ways of achieving the same thing.

Mulching with organic material helps to keep down weed growth around plants and can reduce the risk of disease, it helps the soil retain moisture for longer, it protects the soil from the effects of extreme weather, particularly in winter when heavy rain can literally 'wash' the goodness out of the soil and create a pan on top of it, it increases aeration of the soil due to increased earthworm activity, it will add fertility and improve the texture of soil as it breaks down.

Mulches can also save long term work because weed seedlings are deprived of light and will therefore die. The mulch also creates a barrier which stops weed seeds from reaching the soil in the first place. Mulching prevents surface capping of the soil and helps to maintain a good soil structure. A layer of mulch keeps the soil at an even temperature so that roots do not get scorched and so that the risk of frost damage is reduced. Mulches offer protection to worms; which in turn improve the aeration of the soil. You can use your lawn clippings (as long as they are chemical-free) to mulch peas and beans and any organic mulch like well-rotted manure will also benefit the soil by adding nutrients. The pH balance of the soil can be slightly manipulated by the mulch in as much as spent mushroom compost, composted seaweed or limestone chippings can prevent an acid soil from becoming even more acid. Mulches protect low growing fruit from mud splashes and generally improve the yield and growth rates of all flowers and vegetables.

There are a few disadvantages to using a mulch but most of them can be overcome given a bit of preparation before mulching. Perennial weeds or even little bits of root (couch grass, ground elder, etc.) will flourish beneath a mulch if they are not removed. It is therefore necessary to dig the soil over and weed very thoroughly before applying the mulch. Saturate the soil before mulching since polythene or any waterproof material will prevent the rain from reaching the soil and any absorbent organic mulch will absorb the rain water before it can reach the soil. Straw, wood bark, wood shavings or sawdust (all un-composted) will rob the soil of nitrogen as they decompose. If you are using them as a mulch you will need to treat the soil to a nitrogenous fertilizer before laying the mulch. Remember that mulches can harbour pests, slugs, snails and wireworms, so vigilance is required. Make sure that there is a gap left around plant stems since mulch can cause disease and incom-

Comfrey makes both an excellent liquid fertiliser and a natural mulch.

The best time to apply a mulch is either just after planting, particularly in the case of shrubs and young trees, which need to be given the best possible start without competition from weeds, or when the soil is warm and moist. Never mulch a very cold/very wet/very dry soil – the mulch will prevent the soil from reaching the ideal moisture and heat levels – completely the opposite of what you are trying to achieve!

pletely rotted compost can burn stems and basal leaves.

There are masses of mulching ingredients you can use, your own garden compost being one of the best. If you can't spare this to be used as mulch, then wilted comfrey or nettle leaves are great as they will both suppress weeds then add fertility as they break down into the soil. Straw and hay, any cut leafy material from green manures, leaf mould, spent mushroom compost, seaweed and dried lawn clippings are all suitable for covering the soil.

How much mulch should you use around your plants? If weed suppression is the main aim, then generally the thicker you can apply the mulch, the better. Garden compost needs to be around one inch (2.5cm) deep at least to provide an effective layer but 'fluffier' mulches such as straw, hay and wilted leaves can be applied to at least six inches (15cm) to allow for settling over time.

A mulch layer is also useful for covering the soil between rows of young seedlings. This will suppress the growth rate of any weeds that appear and your precious young plants will be able to grow unhindered. Used between rows of older vegetables it will seal in moisture and again, reduce competition from weeds. Don't forget that mulching is just as important, if not more so, in the polytunnel or greenhouse in the summer to slow down the evaporation of water.

Green Manures

Leaving a bed or border completely bare for long periods of time (particularly over the winter) is very detrimental to the soil. Without any kind of ground cover, whether in the form of plants or mulches, the soil is right in the firing line for all that the weather can throw at it. Heavy rain can literally wash the nutrients from the topsoil, and the soil structure itself can be damaged. Sowing what we call a 'green manure' on any vacant space of soil will protect it until it is needed again. The green manure can then be dug back in, increasing soil fertility as it decays under the soil. There are many benefits to be had from green manures; increasing organic matter and available nitrogen, helping to smother weeds, increasing drought protection, protecting the soil surface and structure, some have flowers and so attract beneficial insects and foliage to protect them and deep-rooting plants extract nutrients from deep down in the soil and these are released when the manure is dug back in. The plant material can also be used as a mulch or added to the compost heap.

A Selection of Green Manures

Alfalfa (Lucerne)

Rich in calcium and the major elements. It is a very deep rooting plant and will bring trace elements to the soil surface. It can be left for several years with the foliage being cut for mulching. Otherwise it can be dug in during autumn or left to stand over the winter.

Agricultural Lupin

Deep rooting and useful for breaking up the soil. Does well in acid soils.

Buckwheat

Lots of fast growing foliage to surpress weeds. Excellent for digging in as it decomposes quickly.

Clovers

There are several different types of clovers and all of them will fix nitrogen in the soil when dug in. Wild white clover is good for growing between rows of plants to suppress weeds as it is low growing, red clover has very strong growth and will produce large amounts of foliage to use as a mulch; once cut back, it will regrow.

Mustard

A very quick growing short term green manure said to help reduce wireworm in the soil. Dig into the soil before flowering. Its deep roots mean it will lift nitrogen and incorporate it into the soil once dug in.

Fenugreek

A summer green manure which can also be eaten as 'greens' and used as a flavouring in cooking.

Phacelia

A very attractive plant, attracting useful insects if allowed to flower. The foliage smothers weeds and its extensive root system is good for breaking up and improving soil structure.

Crop Rotation

I mentioned earlier the importance of moving different types of crops around into different areas or beds each year. This practice has been carried out for a very long time, probably as long as the act of gardening itself, and there are several reasons why it is important. Before we go into any great depth, it is important to recognise the links between closely related plants

Clover (top)
Mustard (middle)
Phacelia (bottom)

and vegetables in order to be able to group them together when planning a yearly rotation. Actually, this rotation is best carried out on a three or four year cycle, or even five to six years if you have the space, as it gives the soil a chance to replenish its nutrients naturally as well as eliminating diseases and pests. Basically the longer the rotation cycle the better, but don't get too worked up if you haven't got the space on your plot to follow this rigorously – using companion planting methods such as intercropping can help enormously in reducing pest and disease problems.

If you are able to divide your vegetable garden up into several separate beds then obviously this will be far easier when you start to grow and rotate your crops year on year. A larger expanse will do just as well, of course, as long as you can define it into sections. One of the most important things about rotations is to make a note of what grew where each year – once a couple of years have passed it is all too easy to forget where you are in the cycle!

Plant Families	
Solanium 	The potato family, which also includes tomatoes, peppers and aubergines.
Legumes 	Peas, beans (broad, runner and French) and clovers
Alliums	Onions, Shallots, garlic and leeks
Brassicas 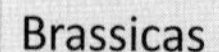 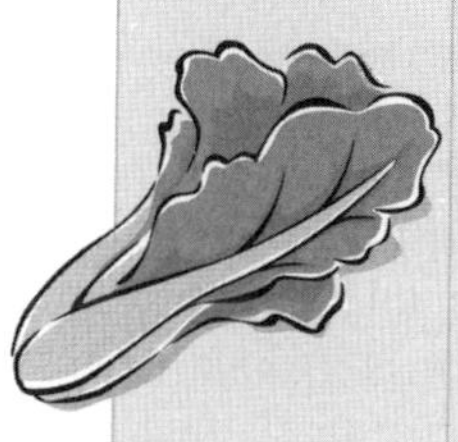	These are members of the cabbage family, some of which may surprise you to learn they are closely related: cauliflower, calabrese, broccoli, Brussels sprouts, kale, cabbage, kohlrabi, Chinese cabbage, radish, turnips, Swedes, salad rocket and many oriental vegetables.
Umbellifers 	Carrots, parsley, parsnips, celery and celeriac.
Some other vegetables are classified individually and can be popped in wherever there is space for them. These are all members of the squash family (marrow, courgette, pumpkin) as well as sweet corn, beetroot, chard and lettuce.	

Soil Fertility

Different crops have differing nutritional needs, and some even have the means of adding fertility to the soil – the legume family (peas and beans) take nitrogen from the atmosphere and store it in nodules on their stems. They are known as 'nitrogen fixers' and once their crops have been harvested, the plants can be dug back into the soil to add nitrogen for the following crop. Bear in mind that longer or shorter root systems on plants take nutrients out of the soil at different levels and varying the crop each year means that this depletion will not occur in the same layer of soil.

Weed Control

Companion planting really has a part to play in a crop rotation where plants with dense foliage are useful for shading the ground underneath them, making it almost impossible for weeds to germinate. Leafy potatoes and squash plants are excellent for this and if in the following year a less bushy plant is grown in the same spot, for example carrots or parsnips, the weed burden should not be so severe.

Not all weeds are bad for the garden. There are many beneficial weeds (or 'wild plants', if you prefer!), which can be allowed to grow alongside plants you have raised, imparting the same kinds of benefits as mixing cultivated crops.

However, not all weeds are bad for the garden. There are many beneficial weeds (or 'wild plants', if you prefer!), which can be allowed to grow alongside plants you have raised, imparting the same kinds of benefits as mixing cultivated crops. A selection of the best ones to use for companion purposes is listed in the A-Z section, but some of the most useful are dandelion, stinging nettle, tansy, thistle, yarrow and wild or hedge garlic. Of course no weed should ever be allowed to become so rampant that it takes over, to the detriment of the plants close to it.

The dandelion, so long viewed as the gardener's enemy, is actually a friend which, when allowed to grow alongside crops, imparts the same benefits as mixing cultivated crops.

Control of Pests and Diseases

Pests and diseases are normally linked to certain groups of plants, for example club root disease in the soil affects brassicas, or nematode pests (eelworm) affect potatoes, and so if susceptible plants are grown in the same soil year on year, these pests and diseases can increase dramatically. Moving each group around on a cycle will reduce the risk of these building up, or of even striking in the first place. For this reason rotation is important not just outside in the garden but even in the greenhouse or polytunnel if the plants are grown directly into soil beds. All this will of course be even more effective if you choose to interplant with suitable companion plants to repel and divert pests away from your vegetables.

There is not really any hard and fast rule for which way round to rotate your crop families, but in a newly cultivated plot, potatoes are excellent for breaking up heavy ground. The tubers will need to be planted in a trench, covered over, then earthed up as the foliage (known as 'haulms') begin to emerge and grow. Then there is the digging up of the crop once the time comes for harvest. You will certainly have well cultivated soil at the end of your first year on your potato bed!

Goodies and Baddies:

Insects, Animals and Avian Friends, Pests and Predators

Companion planting schemes are frequently introduced to attract or repel all sorts of creatures, both friends and foes. This section will help you discover the ways in which you can enhance your garden and achieve your ultimate aims for particular plants, whether you want to lure things in to help your precious plants thrive, or protect them from being attacked and eaten. Companions, good and bad, come in both insect and animal form. Whatever you want to do you can be sure that all these methods are totally natural and won't harm the environment. Tons better than reaching for a chemical spray any day!

A Wildlife Area in your Garden

You could argue that setting aside a piece of your garden solely to attract wildlife could be asking for trouble, for who is to say whether what you attract will be harmful to your plants or not? However, due to the constant threat to our countryside from development and from climate change, gardens are becoming increasingly important. Even though an individual garden may be small, many gardens added together make up a huge area and the land they

cover can be of great importance as potential wildlife habitats.

Our gardens are not just beneficial for all kinds of wildlife, they have now become an essential part of its survival. Starlings, stag beetles, song thrushes, house sparrows and hedgehogs are all declining in numbers in the UK, but these species can benefit enormously if the gardens they inhabit are managed sympathetically. And by doing this we can encourage tremendous diversity and create countless habitat opportunities.

It is not just our wildlife that is under threat. Green gardens are in decline too, as the trend for paving them over has increased. Not only does this deprive creatures of habitats but it can also create serious problems resulting in flooding and possibly increased global warming.

The most rewarding aspect of wildlife gardening is that it is hugely beneficial to nature's biodiversity and at the same time extremely good for your own health, both mentally and physically. So create a little wildlife habitat in your garden and enjoy all the colour, energy and interest it will bring.

Ponds

Make a pond – it doesn't need to be massive. Once you have a pond in your garden you will certainly attract a few frogs or toads and probably both. These useful creatures eat many garden pests, particularly that bane of any gardener's life, the slug. Make sure your pond has at least one rough, gently sloping side to enable any frogs to get out of the water easily. A pond will also attract insects such as dragonflies and allow them to breed. Shallow margins with lots of semi-aquatic plants will provide them with an ideal habitat.

Wildlife 'Hidey-Holes'

A garden doesn't need to be completely overgrown or untidy to be attractive to wildlife; simply providing a couple of areas that provide shelter and a safe haven is quite adequate to draw some interesting and useful creatures in.

Something as simple as a small pile of logs can become a haven for many of our native insects and toads and frogs in particular. You can always find somewhere to put a pile of logs, even in the smallest of gardens. The pile is best placed in a shady spot so that it remains cool and damp. As the wood softens and decays it can also support many different types of fungi. For best results, use a mixture of wood and logs of different sizes with the bark left on, for example beech, oak, ash and elm. Adding a heap of leaf litter in the autumn can attract even more creatures such as hedgehogs and toads, who will use it to hibernate in. As the logs decay over the years, keep adding new ones.

Laying a number of flat stones around the garden will also provide shelter for useful predators like centipedes, ground beetles and toads to name a few; these will then be on hand in your garden to help keep any plant pests under control.

Walls as Wildlife Habitats

Wild solitary bees like the mason bee are so called as they often make their nests between the mortar on old walls. A good population in your garden will ensure the pollination of your garden plants. Re-pointing or repairs to walls should be done carefully and in moderation as gaps in the mortar provide ideal bee nesting sites. South facing sunny walls are much favoured by bees as the bricks or stones provide better heat retention and stay warm long after the sun has gone. Think back to those walled kitchen gardens in Victorian times – the high brick walls achieved the same result and ensured the crops inside the garden thrived in the protected, warmer climate.....and no doubt, there were quite a few bees there too!

Another commonly seen visitor to the garden is the bumble-bee. These are larger and rounder with a furry appearance. They move around more slowly and calmly than smaller bees and are less aggressive; in fact they will only sting if they feel they are really under threat, unlike wasps who sting at the slightest provocation! Male

bumblebees, called drones, don't actually have a sting.

Bumblebees make their nests in places like old mouse nests and banks under hedgerows. These nests are very small in comparison to those of honey bees - up to150 bumble-bees or so per nest, as opposed to a colony of honey bees which can easily reach 50,000 individuals.

It's also a good idea to make sure that you have something in flower all year round so that bees which wake up during spells of warm weather can find a food source. Even in mid-winter, when there is snow on the ground, it is possible to have flowers. Try winter flowering heather, Christmas roses, primroses, snowdrops and winter aconites.

The best flowers for bees of any kind are simple and open as these are more easily accessible to these larger insects. A garden stocked with a wide variety of flowering plants – take for instance a typical English cottage garden – is ideal bee territory.

A good list to start with is foxgloves, hollyhocks, heather, lavender, oregano, cornflowers, honeysuckle, mint, cotoneaster, borage, clover, marigolds and beans.

The main job of bees is to pollinate flowers and a huge amount of all our food is the result of their work. Vegetables like beans rely on bees to pollinate the flowers and without the bees there would be no crops to harvest. We need to safeguard their future - not just for them but for us as well.

Nesting Sites for Bumblebees

As well as helping bees by planting food for them, you can provide places for them to make their nests. Bumblebees use a variety of nesting places – holes in dry banks, walls, under sheds, under large stones and in the leaf litter at the base of hedges. Try to leave some places in the garden undisturbed so that they can find somewhere to build a nest. You could also devise simple winter shelters for them - old plant pots filled with moss and placed on their sides under shrubs are ideal places for wild bees to hibernate.

The queen bee is the only one to survive through the winter and she will find a hole or a sheltered pile of moss or leaves to crawl into for the duration. If you find a solitary queen bee in the cold days of late winter or early spring, try not to disturb her, and gently cover her back up again so she can finish her winter sleep until the temperatures start to warm up in the spring.

Allow clover to grow on the lawn so the bees can feed from the nectar of the flowers. If you don't have a pond, put out large shallow dishes of water with stones in them so that the bees can get a drink - large plant saucers are good for this. They will stand on the stones to get to the water and will also be able to climb out if they fall in.

Honey Bees

For those with a large enough garden there may be some scope to site a beehive or two and begin a new and absorbing hobby keeping honey bees. In recent years the poor old honey bee has struggled against disease, poor weather conditions and drift from chemical sprays and it really needs all the help it can get. Think of all the flowers they will pollinate in your garden and far beyond (a honey bee can travel over 3 miles to gather nectar) and of course the lovely honey you will be harvesting at the end of the season – it all adds up to a very worthwhile venture!

Wild Flower Gardening

A good way of attracting beneficial insects into your garden is to plant wild flowers. These will provide pollen and nectar for bees and butterflies, and larvae (such as caterpillars) often feed on their leaves.

The best place to plant wildflowers is in a sunny spot in the garden, but if you don't have the space you can grow them in a container from seed. Any container will be fine as long as it has drainage holes in the

bottom. Once you've found a suitable container (an old bucket or plastic tub will do) fill it three-quarters full with peat-free compost.

Firm down the soil, sprinkle the seeds on the surface, gently press them in with something flat, then water them. After that you can leave them alone, but do make sure the compost doesn't dry out.

Many wild flower seeds need to be chilled before they germinate so a good time to plant them is in late autumn, so the chilling can be done by Mother Nature over the winter.

There are lots of wild flowers to choose from, for example teasel, thistle, knapweed, lady's bedstraw, meadow buttercup, cowslip, oxeye daisy, black medic, field scabious, self-heal, wild parsnip, wild marjoram, and yarrow. When buying packets of mixed wild flower seed check to make sure that they are all types that are native to the UK and have not been imported from sources overseas. As well as wild flowers, herbs such as rosemary, thyme, sage, basil, sweet marjoram, chives, lovage, lemon balm, parsley, borage and mint will all attract a wide variety of beneficial insects into your garden.

When your plants start to grow you might have to thin them out a little to give them more room, but apart from that you shouldn't have to do any more, except water them from time to time if the weather is dry. Once your wild flowers have finished flowering don't rush to cut them back or pull them up – leave them and let them do as nature intended, and remember, don't be too tidy! Some wild flowers will flower again the following year, others are biennial and will grow one year and flower the next and annuals will self sow and produce new plants next spring.

Many insects will have laid eggs in the compost or hidden amongst the dead stems and leaves to hibernate over winter. Only tidy up small patches of ground at a time rather than all at once so that any bugs will not be left homeless.

Set aside a small area completely untouched which will provide a refuge for many insects and other small creatures.

Include plants that are rich in nectar in your planting schemes. For example Buddleia is well known for attracting nectar feeding insects such as butterflies and hoverflies throughout the summer. In the autumn ivy (Hedera helix) is an excellent source of nectar.

Compost Heaps

Even the tiniest garden needs a compost heap! Put your kitchen scraps and garden waste to good use and make your own wonderful garden compost as well as creating the perfect habitat for many kinds of wildlife. Compost heaps will attract woodlice, millipedes and slugs - essential for breaking down organic and garden refuse! See the earlier section for all the information you need on making and maintaining your own compost heap.

Birds - Feathered Friends or Foes?

It's very difficult to classify birds as a whole as either good or bad for the garden as some are extremely beneficial, while others can wreak havoc on your plants. I believe the odds on the whole are in favour of birds being the gardener's friend rather than his enemy. Beneficial bird species such as the tit family, robins, blackbirds, thrushes, dunnocks and wrens are definitely worth encouraging into the garden. Insect eating birds like these are a very valuable source of natural pest control; blackbirds and thrushes also search out slugs, snails and leatherjackets, (an underground pest and the larva of the cranefly), as do starlings; blue tits eat hundreds of caterpillars and green woodpeckers will eat ants in the grass of lawns.

The decline in woodland areas and older trees means there are fewer nesting sites for over 60 species of birds which use old trees for their nests. Putting up an artificial nest box will help future generations of birds and give you hours of pleasure from watching them. Piles of leaves or logs left in a corner of the garden over the winter will provide homes for insects and these in turn are food for the birds. Shrubs and trees with berries provide a rich source of food in the winter when there is very little else to eat. Water is of course an essential for birds but not only for drinking as even in the coldest weather birds continue to bathe, so a constant water supply all year round is just as important as feeding the birds through the colder months when natural food is

Birds can be both friends and foes.

scarce. That small wildlife pond mentioned earlier is ideal or simply a bird bath made from a shallow bowl.

'Birds - The Dark Side'

Birds can be also responsible for a wide range of damage, some serious, some just plain annoying. In autumn and winter they eat flower buds, strip ornamental berries and attack brassicas. In spring they can destroy flowers, steal seeds and damage seedlings when dust-bathing. Summer damage includes taking fruit and pecking holes in turf.

The worst pests of all (at least on my patch) are pigeons because they really can devastate seedlings in a very short space of time. They have a particular liking for seedlings and freshly planted tender young plants and if they are around when you are sowing seeds such as peas they will probably make a beeline for these as well. Sadly I am not aware of any companion planting schemes that are effective against pigeons!

Pieces of silver foil (or old cds) tied at intervals along lengths of twine attached to sticks and suspended over the beds and borders can make

effective bird scarers, but even then the birds may get used to them eventually. I cover my vulnerable plants and seeds up with nylon netting until they are big enough to stop being tempting to the birds. The netting is not environmentally friendly, but it can be used year after year, and without it I probably wouldn't have any peas and the brassicas would get pecked to pieces.

Our Friends Mr Frog and Mr Toad

I mentioned earlier the importance of a pond in the garden to entice beneficial wildlife, and although both these members of the amphibian family can live out of water, the presence of even the smallest of pools will help keep them in the vicinity of your garden. Frogs and toads will travel considerable distances in search of food which consists of a wide variety of insects, slugs and caterpillars. If you have a greenhouse or polytunnel that is a haven for slugs, then a visit from a frog or toad is always welcome, and they certainly seem quite at home in there – contrary to popular belief they both spend much of their lives on land. You will probably only notice them as you water your plants and they jump out at you from under a leaf! However, frogs and toads do need ponds in which to breed and lay their eggs and the resulting young (tadpoles) stay in the water for three months after hatching – until they have developed legs for life on land.

Hidey holes for these amphibians are essential if you want to keep them in your garden. Logs and stones and wild areas provide shelter and sanctuary for them throughout the year and a place for hibernation in the winter. Public enemy number one for frogs and toads in an urban garden is the domestic cat but they can also fall prey to crows, rats, herons, hedgehogs, foxes and grass snakes.

Another Gardening Ally….the Hedgehog

Hedgehogs are another useful ally to gardeners because they eat slugs, snails and other garden pests. Sadly hedgehog numbers are in decline, in part due to environmental pollution, the loss of their own natural habitats and the huge numbers killed on Britain's roads each year.

The best ways of helping hedgehogs is by providing 'wild' areas in our

gardens, and by not being too tidy. Log and leaf piles are great for hedgehog nests, and in a corner of the garden they will be perfectly placed for a hedgehog hideaway. You could even buy a custom-built hedgehog house and place it in a secluded corner. Hedgehogs are voracious predators of slugs, and so the use of slug pellets containing chemicals should be avoided – these will poison the slugs first, then any hedgehogs unfortunate enough to eat the affected slugs.

Remember also to check bonfire heaps before you light them in case a hedgehog has made his home underneath. When using spades, forks, mowers, strimmers and similar garden tools, check first to see that there are no hedgehogs hiding in close proximity to where you are working to avoid them getting injured. Garden netting can also cause potential problems with hedgehogs getting caught in it: regular checks round the garden each day will ensure all is well.

Mice

Mice can be a real menace, especially in the spring when there are seeds and young tender plants around. They seem to be particularly partial to peas and beans and sweetcorn seed, even when they are buried deep in the soil. Old gardeners were known to soak their seeds in paraffin before sowing them, no doubt to disguise the smell of the seeds. Burrowing can also damage roots and sometimes even kill the plants.

A more environmentally friendly way is to scatter crushed lavender leaves or dried mint leaves over the seed trays or seed beds as mice seem to dislike the strong odour.

Trapping them may seem a cop out but one female mouse can produce from five to ten litters a year with five or six young in each litter. If you live in the countryside then certainly some of these will become welcome meals for owls and other predators, but in town, apart from cats, mice are fairly safe. Humane mousetraps are available to catch mice live, but then you will have the dilemma of what to do with them. Bear in mind that mice can find their way home over long distances! Research has shown that if released less than a mile away, it is very likely that a mouse will find its way home. Over to you...

Rabbits

Happily these cute looking creatures don't usually feature in gardens in the middle of town unless they are safely confined to a hutch and run, but if you live in the countryside or on a town or village margin, then you will know how much damage their wild relatives can cause to your plants. Their voracious and wide-ranging appetites mean they can devastate whole rows of crops in one night. Rabbits are put off by onions and other members of the allium family (leeks, garlic), which they will avoid, so planting rows of these between vulnerable plants should send them hopping off in the other direction. For a truly permanent rabbit-free veg patch you will need to erect an outer fence of wire netting or alternatively you could do as I do and create mini protective tunnels from lengths of wire netting and position them over whichever plants need them most. These can be taken up either when the plants have become too large and tough to be attractive to the rabbits or once the crop has been harvested and used again the following season.

Ladybirds

These useful little beetles are easily recognised by their red, orange or yellow wing cases spotted with black dots. They have a voracious ap-

petite for aphids, scale and other insects, both in their adult state and as larvae. During the larval stage of three weeks, each slate-blue larva will consume several hundred aphids, and even more once it reaches adulthood, so ladybirds are extremely efficient pest controllers. The larvae don't look anything like the adult ladybirds (they are a completely different shape and bizarrely, longer than their parents!), so be careful if you are one for 'squishing' insects on your plants.

Ladybirds hibernate over the winter in sheltered places amongst dense vegetation, leaf-litter, under tree bark etc., or inside buildings, outhouses and sheds. They often invade houses, nestling around doors and window frames, or in the folds of curtains. By far the best place for them is outside, so taking the time to relocate them to a safe shelter for the winter will ensure they are ready for munching their way through a new generation of aphids the following year.

Wasps

Wasps fall somewhere in between the goodies and the baddies, depending on who you are and what you are growing. We all know what a nuisance the common wasp can be in late summer; whenever a sweet drink, ice cream or piece of fruit comes out, a wasp will appear from nowhere! In an orchard wasps can do considerable damage to ripe fruit, particularly if it is sheltered. As a keeper of honey bees I have had complete hives wiped out by marauding wasps at the end of a summer, because they were attracted by the smell of honey in the hives.

In their favour wasps (including the largest British wasp – the hornet, now very rare), spend much of the early part of the year killing insects such as aphids and caterpillars which they feed to their larvae. Other species of wasp parasitise caterpillars and aphids by injecting eggs into them, which hatch and feed on the body tissue of the host. And not least, in the course of their search for all things sweet, wasps do aid pollination.

Wireworms

Shiny, yellowish-orange, stiff-bodied and up to 25mm long, wireworms spend four years in the ground before pupating for three weeks and emerging in the summer as adult click beetles.

They feed on plant roots and bases of stems, ruining potato and other root crops, making tunnels about 3mm in diameter which can later be invaded by slugs or millipedes. Try lifting your maincrop potatoes before September, before the main threat of wireworm damage starts. In the lawn they can weaken the grass, but are not normally a problem. They are usually widespread in grassland, so will be found when it is brought into cultivation. The adult click beetles are brown and elongated, about 15mm long and feed on pollen, nectar and on the tissues of leaves and flowers. When overturned their body makes a "clicking" sound.

Treatments

Crush any wireworms that are found, though they are quite tough to squash. Turning the soil exposes them to birds. Lift crops from infested ground as soon as they mature to avoid damage. Traps can be made using chunks of potato buried in the soil; the wireworms tunnel into the potato which can then be dug up and destroyed.

Carrot Root Fly

It is almost impossible to imagine the problems this tiny insect causes to carrot crops until you have experienced it yourself. This is one major

reason why carrots are not considered an easy crop to grow; in some areas carrot fly attacks reach such proportions that it is common practice to delay seed sowing until mid-July when carrot fly activity is at its lowest. Even then, if you grow carrots you will at some stage have problems with carrot root fly. The flies home in on the smell of the carrots and lay their eggs in the young carrots. The telltale signs are roots riddled with tunnels which turn brown and above ground level the carrot leaves take on a reddish tinge, turning to yellow as the attack gets more advanced. To prevent this, sow as thinly as possible by mixing the seed with silver sand before sowing in the seed drills. This avoids having to thin the carrots out. Normally, breaking the carrot stems when thinning the seedlings creates a lot of scent which attracts the carrot flies.

Cutworms

Cutworms are the larvae (caterpillars) of several species of night-flying moths. The larvae are called cutworms because they cut down young plants as they feed on stems at or below the soil surface. Cutworms attack a wide range of plants including asparagus, beans, cabbage and other brassicas, carrots, celery, sweetcorn, lettuce, peas, peppers, potatoes and tomatoes. If you suspect cutworm, look out for plants cut off near the ground or plants that are noticeably wilting (when cutworms chew on the stems but do not sever the plant). Digging will help to expose the worms and allow birds to eat them and if it is done during the winter it will kill any cutworm larvae in the soil.

Cutworms greatly dislike tansy and can be deterred by having plants growing nearby. Alternatively, crushed fresh leaves and stems can be scattered around the plants you wish to protect. Placing aluminum foil or cardboard collars around transplants will create a barrier that physically prevents cutworm larvae from feeding on your plants. These need to be several inches high and pushed into the ground to prevent the worms burrowing underneath.

Scale Insects

Scale insects are small sap-sucking insects, so called because they produce a waxy coating or 'scale' over their soft bodies. They are more often found on plants grown under protection and telltale signs to look out for are large amounts of sugary honeydew eventually turning into a sooty mould. These characteristics are shared with aphids, and both these pests have a close relationship with ants. By far the best way to stop scale insects arriving in the first place is by keeping areas weed-free as they can provide extra hiding places. Dispose of any leaves that have been removed from an infested plant because these can harbour many recently hatched scales.

Hoverflies

These flies are most easily recognised by their generally bright colours and hovering ability. On first glance they don't look unlike wasps – but they don't sting. The adult hoverflies spend much of their life on flowers, feeding on pollen and nectar, and therefore play an important role in the pollination of many wild and cultivated plants. Hoverfly larvae are voracious eaters of aphids.

Basically just about anything with open, flat topped flowers that supply nectar and pollen will attract hoverflies into your garden.

Lacewings

All lacewings, both as adults and larvae, prey on aphids and other soft-bodied insects and so are great allies to have in the garden.

Aphids

The aphid group comes in several forms; blackfly, greenfly, mealy aphid and root aphid. These little insects smother the young shoots (or roots) of plants and extract the sap which is rich in sugar, hence the reason why the excess is excreted as the sweet honeydew so loved by ants. The leaves can become twisted or blistered after an aphid attack. Aphid predators are described above and are very useful in controlling aphid numbers on plants. Squashing the bugs between finger and thumb is an effective method of instant control as is a spray made from a mixture of soft soap and water.

Butterflies

A colourful butterfly flitting around in a garden is a truly welcome sight, and the majority do no harm at all; in fact they aid pollination, but there are two varieties in particular that give butterflies a bad name in the vegetable garden: the Large White and Small White – more commonly known as 'cabbage whites'. They (or rather their caterpillars) can be serious pests of all members of the brassica

family, hence the common name, but they are also partial to nasturtiums and mignonettes, which can be used as lures to attract the butterflies away from the cabbages.

If you have only a few brassica plants in your garden, netting them so that the butterflies can't reach them to lay their eggs on is the best option. Being vigilant and squashing any butterfly eggs before they hatch is also effective, but you will need to do this on a regular basis and the eggs are tiny and difficult to spot. The caterpillars themselves are easily seen once they hatch and can be picked off before they do too much damage.

Although ants themselves do little damage to plants, they can protect aphids from predators.

Ants

Although ants don't cause damage to plants in a direct sense, they have earned their bad reputation in the garden because of their close connection with aphids. Ants are attracted to sweet food and will often enter houses to forage for sugar. They take nectar from flowers and drink the sap from trees, but one of their favourite food sources comes from aphids, which exude sweet honeydew. The ants go as far as protecting the aphids from predators such as ladybirds, lacewing and hoverfly larvae, and sometimes will even keep an aphid colony in their nest, feeding on roots while the ants 'milk' them for honeydew. Ants will even move aphids and their eggs

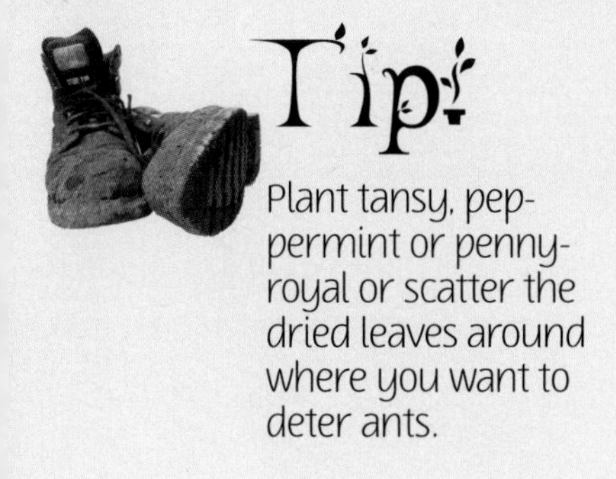

from plant to plant, thereby spreading them around the garden along with any virus they have picked up whilst feeding on affected plants. Ants particularly hate the smell of tansy, peppermint, pennyroyal and southernwood and so the leaves of any of these (fresh or dried) can be liberally scattered around anywhere you wish to deny the ants access.

Spiders

On the whole, spiders should be encouraged into the garden. They do no damage to plants but are predators of many flying and crawling insects – some good, some bad for the garden.

Millipedes

Another insect which has both benefits and disadvantages in the garden. Because they feed on soft plant tissue, millipedes can attack root crops and young plants, but they are also highly beneficial to soil fertility as they recycle dead and decaying leaves. A similar looking insect (but not related) is the centipede which preys on smaller insects such as the woodlouse.

Eelworms

Although some types of eelworms are beneficial, helping to control vine weevils by killing their soil-dwelling grubs, many other kinds are serious and persistent pests which affect a wide range of common garden plants. The best form of control lies in good management, careful selection of the plant stock and ruthless eradication of infected material.

Many herbaceous plants including chrysanthemums and vegetables such as onions, peas, beans, carrots, potatoes, cucumber, lettuce, tomatoes and other salad crops along with soft fruits – most especially

strawberries – are prone to attack by various types of eelworms.

Thrips

Thrips are tiny insects, just 5mm long, often found along veins on the undersides of plant leaves. Damage from thrips often occurs in dry spells, so the first line of prevention should be to supply an adequate amount of water daily, and mulching to hold the moisture in the soil, particular in greenhouses and polytunnels. Signs of thrip damage are dried, mottled silver or brown leaves. Keeping surrounding areas free of weeds will help prevent thrip attack as weed vegetation provides them with an extra habitat. Natural predators are ladybirds.

Fruit Fly

This tiny fly is widespread, more often seen during autumn when it is attracted to ripe fruit. The softer, more delicate fruits, such as plums, apricots and peaches seem to be the most affected. If you have ever made your own wine, you will probably have seen this insect as it is also attracted to the smell of fermenting fruit; if they actually touch the wine, the bacteria carried by the flies can turn it into vinegar.

Strong smelling plants such as southernwood, tansy, eau de cologne mint and basil will help disguise the fruity aroma to a certain extent, but planting these around your trees cannot ever be 100% effective.

Fruit fly has no specific predator. General predators include braconid wasps which are egg parasites, ants and ground beetles which feed on maggots, spiders which catch adults in webs, predatory flying insects such as dragonflies and robber flies and birds such as swallows and wagtails. Increasing the range of habitats available will not give full control but will inevitably give a wide range of benefits.

Poultry are an enormous help in fruit fly control. If you design your orchard to incorporate chickens they will reward you by turning rotten fruit into eggs and will happily spend hours scratching beneath trees looking for fruit fly pupae. Adult fruit flies are trapped on the ground for up to 24 hours after emerging from the pupae as it takes this long for their wings to harden. During this time the adult flies are also vulnerable to a roving hen.

Mealybugs

Early detection of mealybugs is necessary for effective control. Check plants regularly and pay special attention to the new growth, the undersides of leaves and around leaf joints. If the soil is fertile and in good condition, the plants will be well placed to resist the effects of mealybug invasion anyway. Entice natural predators such as ladybirds, hoverflies and lacewings to eat the bugs as soon as they appear.

Mealybugs can also be controlled by rubbing or picking them off affected plants: this works best when infestation is at an early stage and insect numbers are low. You can also prune away and destroy the affected parts. If they have really taken hold you will have to completely remove and destroy heavily infested plants to stop them spreading to other plants.

The A - Z of Companion Plants

APPLES

By far the best companions for apple trees are other apples. Some varieties (and all crab apples) are self-fertile, and if grown in a small group or orchard setting, they will attract far more pollinating insects than one or two trees standing in isolation. Others will need a pollination partner. You just need to make sure that different varieties of tree you buy will flower at the same time; this will ensure pollinators such as bees will travel from one tree to the next, exchanging pollen and ensuring you get a heavy fruit yield.

Orchards are traditionally underplanted with grass which helps suppress unwanted weeds. Just make sure the grass is not allowed to encroach too much, especially if the trees have just been established. Chives planted around can help prevent your tree from forming apple scab. Growing a few nasturtium plants in the vicinity repels codling moth. Foxgloves will help protect your trees from disease, boost their growth and help your apples last longer once they're picked. Other good companion plants for your apple trees are onion, garlic, sweet woodruff and wallflowers.

APRICOTS

Not as tender as they look, but apricots do need a certain degree of shelter from the extreme elements, especially in spring when the trees are in flower. For this reason it's a good idea not to plant them in an area with a cold northerly aspect. Alternatively, a protective shelter belt of hedging will cut down the effects of strong winds. Unlike apples, apricots are self-fertile, so don't need another pollination partner in order to produce luscious, juicy fruit. Basil planted at the base of your apricot tree will help deter fruit flies. The strong scent of garlic and onions planted nearby will keep other pests away. Tansy is great for deterring pests, but use it with caution if you have livestock nearby as it is toxic to animals if eaten. Other good companions for your apricots are asparagus, grapes, onions, southernwood and strawberries.

ARTICHOKE GLOBE

Once seen, these striking giants with their spiking, architectural silver-grey leaves will certainly not be forgotten. They make good companions when used as windbreaks to protect smaller and more delicate plants. The thistle-like flowers of this perennial plant are a great delicacy. A close relative is the cardoon, an heirloom vegetable popular in Victorian times and grown for its stems, which when blanched were eaten like celery, but it has a rather tough texture for modern palates!

ARTICHOKE JERUSALEM

An easy vegetable to grow and extremely useful in the garden, not only because of the edible tubers but the tall stems and leaves can provide a useful protective barrier around more tender plants. It will tolerate most soil types and is great for breaking up previously uncultivated ground in a similar way to potatoes. The stems, which can reach up to 6 feet in a season, will die back over the winter and re-sprout again in the spring, provided of course the tubers have not been dug up for eating! They can be troublesome to clear from an area where they have previously been grown – every single tuber, even tiny or partial ones need to be dug out, otherwise they will re-grow.

ASTER MICHAELMAS DAISY

A real gem of a plant for attracting beneficial insects into the garden. Flowering from mid-summer until late September depending on variety, they are butterfly magnets. Asters are also good companions for asparagus and grow well alongside that old-fashioned perennial, golden rod.

ASPARAGUS

Asparagus is a long-lived perennial that traditionally is planted in its own dedicated bed, each plant widely spaced apart in rows. Applying a mulch to the dormant plants over the winter will protect the crowns and provide nutrition in the following season. Tomatoes make good companions for them as they ward off asparagus beetles. Planting outdoor tomatoes in late spring between the asparagus rows will help your later crops repel the beetle population which usually gets worse towards the end of the cropping season. It is a pity tomatoes aren't hardier, as they could be more useful earlier in the season. Another good companion for asparagus is parsley; both plants derive the mutual benefit of increased vigour.

One of its worst enemies is grass and other invasive weeds. An asparagus bed should be kept weed-free at all times, especially in spring and early summer when the young shoots (spears) are emerging. An impenetrable mat of weeds will make them distort or prevent their breaking through the soil surface at all. Growing companion vegetables or herbs between the rows, such as dill, coriander, tomatoes, parsley, basil, comfrey and marigolds will maximize the available space and make it more difficult for the unwanted weeds to take over. Asparagus does have its dislikes and doesn't get on with onions, garlic and potatoes.

ALFALFA LUCERNE

This is a perennial that roots deeply and fixes the soil with nitrogen and accumulates trace elements such as iron, magnesium, phosphorus and potassium. It withstands droughts with its long taproot and can improve just about any type of soil. Alfalfa has the ability to break up hard clay. It is practically pest and disease free and its foliage can be cut to use as mulch. Very reliable and versatile when used as a green manure.

AMARANTH

A tropical annual that needs hot conditions to flourish, but it can be grown in protected conditions in a polytunnel or greenhouse. Good with sweetcorn, its leaves provide shade giving the corn a rich, moist root run. It is a host to (beneficial) predatory ground beetles. You can eat the young leaves in salads.

ANISE

A liquorice flavored herb and a good host for predatory wasps which prey on aphids. It deters pests from brassicas by camouflaging their odour and improves the vigour of any plants growing near it. Traditionally used in ointments to protect against insect stings and bites. Especially good to plant with coriander.

ARTEMISIA

(varieties: southernwood, wormwood)

These members of the Artemisia family are both extremely effective in repelling all sorts of insects and have been widely used for centuries. As useful inside the house as outside it, the leaves can be used to repel moths, fleas, mosquitoes, slugs and mice. A brew made with crushed leaves and boiling water, then strained and cooled, makes an effective rinse for cats and dogs to rid them of fleas. This 'tea' can also be used to deter slugs and even mice – simply spray it over the areas they frequent and they will steer clear of them. The toxicity produced in its roots means that other plants in close proximity fare badly.

AUBERGINE EGGPLANT

Plant this with amaranth, beans, peas, spinach, tarragon, thyme and marigold. Aubergines are a member of the nightshade family along with tomatoes and potatoes, so do well with peppers. Avoid planting fennel nearby.

BASIL

Pungent, appearing in various forms and a delicious addition to salads and especially delicious when eaten with tomatoes, basil is truly one of the very best companions you can have for repelling unwanted pests. It is also, to my mind, THE smell of summer; clove-like and spicy. There are indeed many different varieties, but sweet, purple and bush basil all carry the scent that repels insects such as aphids, whitefly, mosquitoes, thrips, fruit and house flies. Fortunately, useful insects like bees don't seem to mind it. It is a tender annual, but can be planted outside from spring onwards; however, it really comes into its own under cover in a greenhouse or polytunnel, where it can be planted in amongst its great friend the tomato, to protect it against whitefly. Basil will also improve the tomato's growth and enhance the flavour of the fruit. So these two are truly good companions: both as plants and also on the plate.

A bad companion for basil is the herb rue. Both strong smelling and repellent to flies, it has long been noted that they do not thrive when planted closed together. Rue dislikes sage too, but it does have its uses in keeping unwanted insects away. Rue sap can cause skin irritation so care is needed when handling it. Plant basil with tomatoes to improve their growth and flavour. Basil also does well with peppers, oregano, asparagus and petunias.

BAY

The strong scented leaves so useful in flavouring stews and sauces have been found to protect stored flours and grain products from insects. Bays can grow into quite large shrubs and are hardier than their Mediterranean appearance suggests. I have one in my garden that is in a very exposed position and now stands over 7 feet tall. Try training an annual climber up it to create a striking feature. A fresh leaf bay leaf in each storage container of beans or grains will deter weevils and moths. Sprinkle dried leaves with other deterrent herbs in the garden as a natural insecticide dust. A good planting combination is bay, cayenne pepper, tansy and peppermint.

For ladybird invasions try spreading bay leaves around in your house anywhere they are getting in and congregating. This should persuade them to leave or you could gently relocate them yourself to prey on any aphids in your greenhouse!

BEANS LEGUMES

French, broad and climbing beans, and also peas, are all members of the legume family. They all possess an important attribute; the ability to fix nitrogen in the soil. The brilliant thing with beans is that once the crop has been harvested, the foliage can be incorporated back into the soil to break down and the nitrogen stored in nodules on their roots will be released back into the earth. Other examples of legumes are clover, alfalfa, common vetch and fenugreek (see the green manure section for more information). All beans enrich the soil with nitrogen fixed from the air. In general they are good company for carrots, celery, chards, corn, aubergine, peas, potatoes, brassicas, beets, radish, strawberries and cucumber. Beans are great for heavy nitrogen users like sweetcorn and grain plants because of their nitrogen fixing ability, so the nitrogen used up by the sweetcorn and grains are replaced at the end of the season when the bean plants die back. French haricot beans, sweetcorn and melons are a good planting combination. Summer savory deters bean beetles and improves growth and flavour. But remember to keep beans away from the alliums (onions, chives, garlic).

BEETROOT

Underestimated, in my opinion, the beetroot is a versatile vegetable and easy to grow. Both its leaves and roots can be eaten and it is relatively trouble-free with regard to diseases and pests. Many of the traditional red varieties have attractive deep purple leaves which would not look out of place in a flower border. Also look out for the golden, white and red/white varieties. Beetroot grows best with other members of the beet family: Swiss chard, leaf beet and perennial spinach, as well as kohlrabi, onions, dwarf beans, lettuce, cabbage and other members of the brassica family. I have found they do not grow well with runner or other tall climbing beans; the competitiveness of the taller plants seems to make them struggle. The main pests of beetroot are birds (young seedlings are most at risk) and slugs, which can attack the tops of the roots during a spell of damp weather.

BORAGE

This a fantastic annual plant to attract bees into your garden and so excellent sited in the vicinity of fruit trees. Similar to comfrey in that it is rich in plant nutrients, so when the flowers have finished the leaves can be harvested and scattered around the vegetable plot. A good companion for strawberries, tomatoes and squash in particular, although most plants grown close to it will benefit from it as it increases their resistance to pests and diseases. Borage is an annual and will self-seed to come up the following year if you let it. The attractive blue star-shaped flowers are edible and make a striking decoration to any summer drink or dessert.

BRASSICAS

Brassica is the family name for all members of the cabbage family. These are broccoli, Brussels sprouts, cauliflower, calabrese, cabbage, kale, turnip, kohlrabi and radish. It is important to identify them all as crop rotation for this family is very important. Club root can be a big problem in the soil if brassicas are grown on the same patch of soil and is very difficult to eradicate if you have it as the clubroot spores can survive in soil for up to 20 years. Annual rotation, improving drainage and raising the pH level of your soil will help to keep your soil free of it. Mulching the soil surface will also help. Young brassicas can suffer badly from flea beetles when first planted or when the young seedlings first emerge after sowing. They seem to have a penchant for tender young radishes anyway! Telltale signs are uneven edges of leaves where the insects have eaten them. Keeping the soil moist in the early stages seems to deter the flea beetles. Brassicas are heavy feeders and need a rich soil with plenty of lime. Avoid planting them close to mustards and members of the nightshade family (tomatoes, peppers, etc.). Because brassicas often suffer from attacks from whitefly, aphids and the caterpillars of cabbage white butterflies, planting closely with strong smelling neighbours such as thyme, rosemary, mint, sage, and chamomile should throw these pests off their quest to lay eggs on your plants! Planting a group of nasturtiums as a sacrificial crop will tempt grey aphids away from your brassicas, then they can be dealt with by squashing between finger and thumb or by spraying with a soap solution. Other good neighbours for brassicas are onions, garlic and chives.

BROCCOLI SEE BRASSICAS

BRUSSELS SPROUTS SEE BRASSICAS

BUCKWHEAT

This fast-growing ground cover crop accumulates calcium and produces masses of foliage to suppress weeds. If you allow it to flower, it will attract hoverflies in droves.

CABBAGE SEE BRASSICAS

CALABRESE SEE BRASSICAS

CARAWAY

Good for loosening compacted soil due to its deep roots and also compatible next to shallow rooted crops. Caraway benefits strawberries when planted next to them, but it can be tricky to establish. The flowers attract a number of beneficial insects, especially the tiny parasitic wasps. Keep it well away from dill and fennel.

CARROTS

Carrots come in many forms, not just the ones with the pointed orange roots! Try a change by growing some purple, red or yellow, stump rooted or round ones. Whatever varieties you choose, the flavour of your home-grown carrots will be far tastier than anything you will buy in the shops. Carrots do best in fine, deep, well-drained, stone free soil that's free of weeds. Weeding around tiny carrot seedlings is a tedious and thankless task, believe me! If you are going to dig in any compost or well-rotted manure, make sure this is done several months before you need to sow your carrots. Freshly manured soil (and soil with a lot of stones in it) tends to make the carrots fork and distort.

A serious and widespread pest of carrots is the carrot root fly and it is a very lucky gardener whose carrots never fall prey to this tiny insect. To this end, the very best companions for carrots are plants that will repel by their strong scent, such as the allium family (leeks and onions) and also herbs such as sage, rosemary and wormwood. A heritage vegetable, scorzonera, also makes an effective barrier. A thick 'wall' of any of these plants will send the carrot root fly in another direction, even better if the companions can be mingled in amongst the carrots as well. Carrot flies can detect the smell of carrot from long distances and so care needs to be taken when thinning young seedlings (cut rather than pull them out) and carefully firm the soil back down afterwards, and also after harvesting. Certain varieties of carrots bred to be resistant/less attractive to carrot root fly are available, and this will cut down fly attack to a certain extent, but will never stop it completely. A combination of resistant carrot varieties plus a protective barrier planting is the canniest option.

The number one bad companion is cow parsley, not because of adverse effects it has on carrots, but because they are closely related and so can also harbour carrot root fly which migrates once the cow parsley comes into flower. Other friends for carrots are leaf lettuce and tomatoes. Keep dill and parsnips away from them.

CATNEP CATMINT NEPETA

An effective deterrent for flea beetles, aphids, ants and weevils, it can also repel mice: just spread some sprigs of catmint in areas you want the mice to avoid. Use sprigs of catmint or catnep anywhere in the house you want to deter both mice and ants. It imparts a strange but not unpleasant smell and is of course very natural.

CAULIFLOWERS SEE BRASSICAS

Another member of the cabbage family and so all the previous information applies to the cauliflower. The varieties with coloured flowering heads (curds) are really attractive enough to be planted along the edge of a flower border. Look out for maroon and lime green. Caulis need a moist soil for the heads to develop properly, so keep them well-watered in dry spells. A variety called 'Romanesco' is lovely, with a pale green turreted head – it's absolutely delicious too! Avoid planting tomatoes and strawberries nearby.

CELERY

Celery has a strong scent which many insects dislike and so rarely suffers any damage. The main pest is the celery leaf miner which can be fooled by growing leeks as companions to repel them. Leeks make excellent companions for celery as their soil requirements are similar: rich, moist soil with a high alkaline content (6.5).

It is also useful grown in close proximity to any members of the brassica family as cabbage white butterflies seem in particular to avoid it. Celery likes a humous-rich, well manured soil with plenty of moisture as it originally grew in marshy areas. Other good companions are tomatoes, dill, spinach and all members of the legume (bean) family. Celery also favours certain flowers as companions, such as antirrhinums, cosmos and daisies. It dislikes sweetcorn.

CELERIAC

A root vegetable that really does smell and taste just like celery. Extremely versatile, the root bulb can be boiled, grated raw on salads, puréed or made into soup and the leaves can be used as an alternative to celery in many recipes. It suffers little from pest and disease damage and slugs can be discouraged by growing leeks alongside.

CHAMOMILE

A strongly scented herb, renowned for making tea. This annual plant can improve the flavour of cabbages, cucumber and onions. It is a popular host to hoverflies and wasps and accumulates calcium, potassium and sulphur, later returning them to the soil. It can increase oil production from herbs. Roman chamomile is a low growing perennial that will tolerate almost any soil conditions. All chamomile varieties thrive in full sun. Growing chamomile of any type is considered a tonic for anything you grow in the garden.

CHERVIL

A delicate, feathery-leafed herb that is a good companion to radishes, lettuce and broccoli for improved growth and flavour. It will keep aphids off your lettuces and has been used to deter slugs. Plant it thickly amongst the plants you wish to protect, if possible choosing a reasonably shady spot which will suit it nicely.

CHIVES

Not surprisingly, this pungent smelling onion-like herb has very few enemies in the way of pests and diseases! It grows well with apples, carrots, tomatoes, brassicas (broccoli, cabbage, mustard, etc.) and many others. It helps to keep aphids away from tomatoes, chrysanthemums, sunflowers and many other plants prone to aphid attack. Planted among apple trees it helps prevent scab and among roses it prevents black spot. This is a long term measure as it takes about 3 years for plantings of chives to prevent the 2 diseases, so patience will be needed. A tea made from an infusion of chives may be used on cucumber and gooseberries to prevent downy and powdery mildews. Avoid planting them near beans and peas.

CLOVER

(also see the entry for 'green manures' in section 2)

Long used as a green manure and plant companion, it is especially good to plant under grapevines. Clover flowers attract many beneficial insects and are particularly attractive to bees. Useful planted around apple trees to attract predators of the woolly aphid. Clover interplanted with cabbage has been shown to reduce the number of pests because it attracts large numbers of the predators that feed on them.

COMFREY

Every organic garden should have a patch of comfrey. It makes excellent liquid fertiliser and the potash, nitrogen and phosphate-rich leaves are perfect to use as a mulch around plants and to line planting holes for tomatoes and trenches for potatoes. The plants themselves are highly invasive, however, and really need a dedicated area to themselves. Properly looked after they can be harvested 3 or 4 times a year and can live up to 20 years. They need plenty of water to keep them growing on throughout the summer months – harvesting of the leaves and stems for mulch or fertilizer needs to be done before the plants come into flower, otherwise the leaves become very sparse. Comfrey is beneficial to most fruit trees and is a traditional medicinal plant. A good trap crop for slugs.

CORIANDER

Another strong smelling herb, coriander has an unusual, not altogether unpleasant scent, but one that is repellent to many insects, in particular aphids and spider mites. The flowers, however, are highly attractive to bees so it is useful for luring them over to any other plants you want pollinating. A tea made from coriander can be used as a spray against spider mites. A good growing partner for anise, chervil and dill, which used together in a group planting will prevent pests homing in on your carrots and brassicas. Coriander and fennel are mortal enemies and each one has a negative effect on the other.

CUCUMBER

No question, in the United Kingdom climate the cucumber is more reliable under cover in a greenhouse or polytunnel where they can be cosseted and protected from the elements. The F1 hybrid varieties have been bred for indoor cultivation and are the ones to look out for if you are going to grow them inside. For the great outdoors, however, choose one of the hardy varieties such as 'Marketmore.' and 'Burpless Tasty Green'. These are great to plant with sweetcorn and beans as the three plants like the same conditions: warmth, rich soil and plenty of moisture. Train the cucumbers to grow up and over your sweetcorn plants. A great combination is to plant cucumbers with sunflowers. The sunflowers provide a strong support for them. Cucumbers also do well with peas, beets, radishes and carrots. Radishes are a good deterrent against cucumber beetles. Dill planted with cucumbers helps by attracting beneficial predators. Nasturtium improves their growth and flavour. Keep sage and rue away from them.

DANDELION

These little plants are so useful, it's a pity that so many people think of them as a bad thing to have in their gardens. My dad used to make the most amazing wine from the flowers, and I use the leaves sparingly in salads; the young tender leaves spice up a mixed salad. If you really have to dig them up, then these copper-rich plants can be added to your compost heap where they will decompose and add valuable nutrients to the mix. Because of its long root system, the dandelion can lift nutrients and minerals from deep within the soil, and the roots help to break up heavy soils, particularly when the plants die, leaving air spaces in the soil where the mass of roots once were. It is known that dandelions give off ethylene gas, similar to bananas, which can cause both fruits and flowers to mature quickly. Bear this is mind if they are present in an orchard.

DILL

Dill is a dainty, feathery leafed herb grown mainly for adding to fish dishes, but it is also able to offer many benefits to the organic gardener. The cabbage white butterfly hates it and so it is useful planted amongst the cabbage patch, especially as it also seems to stimulate growth and improve disease resistance. If allowed to flower, dill will attract honeybees. Other companion plants that derive benefit from dill include cucumbers, cabbage, sweetcorn, melons, onions and lettuce. It deters flying pests away from carrots and tomato plants in its early stages of growth, but hinders their progress if left in the ground to mature and flower, so is another candidate for the compost heap when it has served this purpose. It also improves the growth and health of cabbage. It attracts hoverflies and predatory wasps and repels aphids and spider mites to some degree.

ELDERBERRY

If you think of the humble elderberry as a 'weed' tree, then it may surprise you to learn that it has many beneficial attributes and can be extremely useful in the garden. A spray made from the leaves can be used against aphids, carrot root fly, cucumber beetles and peach tree borers. Put branches and leaves in mole runs to banish them. Elderberry leaves added to the compost heap also speed up the decomposition process.

FENNEL

Fennel and dill look very alike as young plants, having similar foliage, and grow alongside each other quite happily. Unfortunately, many other plants seem to hate fennel which is a pity as insects give it a very wide berth; otherwise it could make a very effective repellent. If allowed to seed it can become a nuisance, being very invasive. The seeds are useful for flavouring herbal tea and the crushed pungent scented leaves make a fantastic home-made flea repellent for your pets.

FOXGLOVE

The foxglove is a biennial member of the figwort family, having been native to the UK since the fifteenth century. Growing the old-fashioned purple foxglove (digitalis purpurea) near potatoes and tomatoes stimulates growth and protects them against fungus disease. Foxgloves are also good planted near apple trees for the same reasons, with the added benefit that their influence improves the keeping quality of the apples. Being a woodland plant, the foxglove prefers the dappled shade created by a tree's leafy canopy, so an orchard setting suits it well. The flowers are very attractive to bees, but all parts of the foxglove are highly poisonous. Having said that, it plays an important part in modern medicine for heart conditions, being the plant from which digitalin is extracted for treating heart disease.

GARLIC

Plant a few garlic bulbs near roses to repel aphids. It is also a good companion for apples, pears, cucumbers, peas, lettuce and celery. A natural accumulator of sulphur, a naturally occurring fungicide, garlic will help to ward off disease in the garden. This is taken up by the plant's pores and if a garlic infusion is used as a soil drench it is also taken up by the roots. Garlic has a negative effect on members of the bean (legume) family, however, because the sulphur can kill beneficial bacteria in the soil which beans use to 'fix' the nitrogen they need to promote healthy growth. Garlic is effective for repelling aphids, codling moths, snails, and carrot root fly. Researchers have observed that time-released garlic capsules planted at the bases of fruit trees actually kept deer away. Further proof of its effectiveness as a pest controller is confirmed by concentrated garlic sprays having been observed to repel and kill whiteflies and aphids, among others, with as little as a 6-8% concentration.

GARLIC WILD OR HEDGE

When crushed the leaves and stems do indeed smell very strongly of garlic and thus are useful in the same way as ordinary garlic. It grows best in moderately shaded areas and so is best planted underneath leafy companions to protect them from aphid infestations, rather than on an open site which would not suit them at all.

GERANIUM

The strong aromatic scent of geranium leaves is unmistakable and certainly not a favourite of many insect pests. It is a great plant for masking the scent of others and repels all sorts of bugs and beetles, but is particularly useful for protecting grapevines from beetles, so if you have some space, plant several around the vines, and also around roses, sweetcorn, tomatoes, peppers and cabbage. Geraniums also help to distract leafhoppers, carriers of several viral diseases.

GRAPES

Hyssop is beneficial to grapevines as are basil, beans, geraniums, oregano, clover, peas, or blackberries. Radishes and cabbage need to be kept away from them, however. Planting clover nearby will increase the soil fertility which the grapes will appreciate. Chives will help repel aphids. Good tree companions for grapevines are said to be elm and mulberry: the elm is rather a large tree to be grown in a regular size garden for the sake of a vine, but a mulberry is more manageable as it grows very slowly. Train a vine up the mulberry and use the space to great effect – two crops for the price of one.

GROUND ELDER

This is a very difficult weed to eradicate from the garden as its spreading roots can quickly cover a large area, shooting up new growth as it does. It is similar to couch grass in that to eradicate it completely you will need to painstakingly dig out every single piece of root. If it is underneath an established hedge or in a shrub border then you have problems! Mexican marigolds (tagetes Minuta) planted close by inhibit the growth of ground elder and this, coupled with removing as much of the root as you can, will eventually help you win the battle again this invasive plant.

HORSERADISH

A wild, hardy plant which is often seen growing on wasteland and along roadside verges. The strong tasting horseradish sauce made from it needs no introduction. Horseradish increases the disease resistance of potatoes and there are some very effective insect sprays that can be made with the root. Fruit trees and apples in particular, benefit from its fungus resistant properties. It is very invasive and so the roots need to be restricted if it is not going to get out of hand. Plant individual roots in bottomless plastic pots to prevent the roots spreading.

HOREHOUND

Like many varieties in the mint family, the many tiny flowers attract many different beneficial flying insects. The larval forms of these insects parasitize or consume many other insect pests. It grows where many others fail to thrive and can survive harsh winters. Flowering over a long season, it will attract beneficial insects almost as long as you are likely to need them. For best results use horehound directly as a companion plant. It stimulates and aids fruiting in tomatoes and peppers.

HYSSOP

A companion plant to cabbage and grapes, hyssop will deter cabbage moths and flea beetles. All flower colour variations (blue/pink/white) are effective. Hyssop is one of the top bee plants and some beekeepers have been known to rub the hive with it to encourage the bees to keep to their home. Hyssop forms a nice compact plant and is not invasive, so makes a great candidate for interplanting. However, don't plant it near radishes.

KOHLRABI SEE ALSO BRASSICAS

This unusual looking vegetable is a member of the brassica family – not so strange as its root looks like a turnip with 'greens' growing out of the top of it! Good for planting with cucumbers, onions and chives. But the very best combination for kohlrabi is beetroot. Don't plant kohlrabi with climbing beans, peppers strawberries or tomatoes.

LARKSPUR

An annual member of the delphinium family, larkspur attracts many insect pests. Unfortunately for them, but luckily for us, larkspur is poisonous, so think of it as nature's insecticide. Just as beautiful outside in a cottage garden or as a striking flower arrangement in a vase indoors.

LAVENDER

Its strong perfume repels fleas and moths. Most varieties do the same job, but lavender vera is the old English variety. Prolifically flowering lavender attracts and nourishes many nectar feeding and beneficial insects. It can also protect nearby plants from insects such as whitefly, and lavender planted under and near fruit trees can deter the codling moth. Use dried sprigs of lavender to repel them. Lavender is easy to propagate from cuttings and far cheaper than buying lots of plants to use around your garden for companion planting. Lavender cuttings can be taken in the autumn, grown on over the winter and planted out the following year. Alternatively you can grow your plants from seed, but you will need more than a little patience as lavender is notoriously slow to germinate!

LEEKS

A member of the allium family. Use leeks near apple trees, carrots, celery and onions which will improve their growth. As with all the members of the allium family, leeks also repel carrot root flies. Leeks and members of the legume family don't grow well in close proximity.

LEMON BALM

A pungently lemon-scented perennial herb with small green or variegated leaves. Sprinkle the dried crushed leaves throughout the garden to deter many bugs that dislike its citronella scent. If you allow lemon balm to flower it will encourage bees into your garden. It makes an effective balm tea that is beneficial for headaches.

LETTUCE

Does well with beets, bush beans, climbing beans, cabbage, carrots, cucumbers, onions, radish and strawberries. Lettuce requires water and lots of it in the summer months, and strong sunlight will scorch its tender leaves. It grows happily in the shade under young sunflowers and climbing beans. Slugs and snails are a real menace where lettuce is concerned, but they hate to travel over very dry and sharp material, so sand, grit, crushed eggshells, coarse ashes and bran can be placed around the plants you want to protect.

LOVAGE

Improves the flavour and health of most plants. It makes a good habitat for welcome ground dwelling insects such as ground beetles. Lovage will grow into a large plant, so a single specimen used as a companion is probably best. Pick the fresh young leaves throughout the year to add to the salad bowl – it tastes similar to celery.

MARIGOLD FRENCH AFRICAN MEXICAN

The little marigold has earned a lot of well-deserved credit as a pest deterrent and in the world of companion planting is second to none. It keeps soil free of bad nematodes (eelworms) and its strong, pungent scent discourages many unwanted insects, particularly whitefly. Generous planting all around the garden and in greenhouses/polytunnels will reap benefits, and the cut leaves and stems can also be used as an insect repelling mulch. Marigolds are very easy and inexpensive to raise from seed, and once you have grown them you will be able to save seed from one year to the next. A natural marigold spray can be made which will help plants resist fungal diseases, for example blight on potatoes and tomatoes. Fresh marigold leaves and stems are crushed and added to a bucket of water and left to stand for a week and given a stir every day or so. By this time the plant material will have started to decompose and the liquid needs to be strained off and retained. Dilute this liquid with exactly the same amount of water mixed with soft soap, pour the mixture in a hand sprayer and it is ready to use. It is best applied as a preventative measure before any symptoms are seen on your plants and it will help them to resist mildews and blight.

FRENCH MARIGOLDS TAGETES PATULA

French marigolds have roots that excrete a substance that kills soil nematodes (eel-worms), and for the best effect the more plants you grow the better. Studies have shown that this nematode killing property remained in the soil for several years after the plants were gone. Mexican marigolds (Tagetes minuta) are the most powerful of the insect repelling marigolds and it is said it can even inhibit weed roots such as bind weed. It will repel many insect pests and even rabbits. Mexican marigolds can have a negative effect on some plants like beans and cabbage, so it is best to grow them well away from each other.

MARJORAM

As a companion plant this herb improves the flavour and growth of most vegetables and herbs. Compact and sweet marjoram are popular varieties and can easily be grown from seed or divided up every three years or so from larger plants.

MELON

Ideal companions are sweetcorn, pumpkin, radish and squash. Other suggested helpers for melons are marigolds, nasturtiums and oregano for providing general pest protection.

MINT

This popular perennial deters white cabbage butterflies, ants, rodents, flea beetles, fleas, aphids and improves the health of cabbages and tomatoes. It really doesn't get on with parsley. You can use cut stems and leaves as a mulch around members of the brassica family. Mint attracts hoverflies and predatory wasps and earthworms are quite attracted to it as well. Having said how useful it is, be careful where you plant it as mint is incredibly invasive. To be on the safe side you might want to keep it contained in a large pot – at least that makes it easily portable too! If you have a mouse problem, then placing mint (fresh or dried) where they run is effective in keeping them away.

MORNING GLORY

A powerful attractant plant for hoverflies and a great growing cover-up for anywhere you want to hide – all morning glories are annuals, so they grow very fast!

MULBERRY

The black mulberry is said to be useful as a decoy crop to entice birds away from other fruit ripening at the same time, but you could argue that once the mulberries are gone your other fruit may become their next target! However, some insect eating birds are also very likely to feast on flying pests and so are well worth attracting.

NASTURTIUM

Fast growing nasturtiums are annuals and easily raised from seed; just sprinkle on the soil where you want the plants to grow in spring and firm in, or sow seed in individual pots for planting out in their final positions later. Don't worry that your soil is too poor for them: they positively thrive in difficult soil conditions. The nasturtium holds an almost unique position in companion planting as it can act both as a repellent against certain plant pests and also be used as a trap crop to attract other pests away from the plants you want to protect (see section on trap cropping). They are effective when planted as a protection barrier around tomatoes, cabbages, cucumbers and under fruit trees. Radishes in particular are ideal companions, improving their flavour, but don't plant them near cauliflowers. Nasturtiums deter wooly aphids, whiteflies and in particular pests of the cucurbit (cucumber, melons, squash) family which makes them ideal for growing under glass or inside polytunnels. They are a great trap crop for blackfly which are especially attracted to the bright orange and yellow flowering varieties. If you have an orchard or even just a fruit tree or two, planting nasturtiums every year in the root vicinity of fruit trees will allow the trees to take up the pungent odour of the plants and repel bugs. The leaves, flowers and seeds of nasturtiums are all edible and add a wonderful peppery flavour to salads. There are several suitable nasturtium varieties available: 'Alaska', 'Tom Thumb Mixed', 'Whirlybird Mixed' and 'Trailing Mixed'.

NETTLES STINGING

How many countless gardening hours have been spent trying to eradicate this useful plant? Granted, if left to its own devices the stinging nettle's root system can spread rapidly, turning a patch of ground into a nettle bed in a relatively short space of time. The old adage that rampant nettles are an indication of fertile soil may not be of much consolation if you have the task of clearing an expanse of nettles! But if allowed their own little space somewhere, nettles can soon prove their worth if used to your advantage. Nettle flowers attract bees and they are an important food source for butterflies. Many of our most colourful and well known species depend on nettles for the growth of their larvae, in particular the red admiral, small tortoiseshell, peacock and the comma.

Sprays made from nettles are rich in silica and calcium which invigorates plants and boosts their disease resistance. Adding a quantity of comfrey leaves into the mixture improves the liquid feed even more. Nettles also impart the same properties to neighbouring plants when grown in close proximity and help ward off nasties such as aphids, mildew and blackfly - if you can tolerate a little wildness in your garden!

ONIONS ALLIUM

One of the most effective companions for disguising others. As well as benefiting others, onions are protected themselves from their arch enemy thrips when grown amongst different plants. Intercropping onions and leeks with your carrots confuses the carrot root fly and planting chamomile and summer savory with onions improves their flavour.

Other companions are carrots, leeks, leaf beet, kohlrabi, strawberries, brassicas, dill, lettuce and tomatoes. Onions planted with strawberries will also strengthen the fruits against disease. Bad companions come in the form of peas and asparagus.

OREGANO

This can be used with most crops but is especially good for cabbage. Plant near broccoli, cabbage and cauliflower to repel the cabbage white butterfly and other flying pests and close to cucumbers to repel cucumber beetles. Closely related wild marjoram (oregano vulgare) will have the same effect. In the garden both plants have a beneficial effect on their neighbours.

PARSNIPS

These are very hardy vegetables and will stand through the winter in the soil ready to be harvested as and when you want them. They are a trouble-free crop in general but can suffer from canker in dry weather if not kept watered, and celery fly and carrot root fly can also prove to be a problem in some areas. The damage from insects is not usually as serious as on carrots, but protection in the form of an onion or leek barrier is a wise move. Because they get on well with carrots and celery, why not plant them all closely and your onion barrier will protect all three crops. As parsnips are slow to germinate and grow on, the interplantings will also help to suppress any weeds. Parsnips thrive in the company of potatoes, radish, peas, peppers, garlic and of course leeks and onions.

PEACH

As with apricots, peaches are tougher trees than the look of their exotic fruit would have you believe! Providing a reasonably sheltered environment will cut down strong winds – the greatest enemy early in the year when the peach blossom is out. Later in the year, once the fruits are formed and ripening, the threat comes from insects like the fruit fly.

Tansy is a perfect insect deterrent and other strong smelling plants grouped around the trees such as southernwood or basil will help disguise the smell of ripening fruit .

PEAR

Similar to apples, some varieties of pear are self-fertile while others will need a pollination partner. Underplanted with grass, so long as it is kept short, the trees will be fine – our own orchard bears out the truth in that: good pear crops year after year. The foxglove, a great companion for trees, is an ideal neighbour. If your pear trees are in an exposed site, a shelter belt of hedging around the plot will provide them some protection from the elements, particularly in spring when they are at their most vulnerable.

PARSLEY

Parsley is a biennial, so you will benefit from its companion planting properties for up to two years. Its allies are asparagus, carrots, chives, onions, roses and tomatoes. Sprinkle the leaves on tomatoes and asparagus. Use as a tea to ward off asparagus beetles. Let some go to seed to attract beneficial insects like tiny parasitic wasps and hoverflies. Parsley increases the fragrance of roses when planted around their base and helps suppress weeds. Mint and parsley are enemies so keep them well away from one another.

PEAS

Like other members of the legume family, peas fix nitrogen in the soil, adding to its fertility. Good companions for peas are bush beans, climbing beans, carrots, celery, chicory, sweetcorn, aubergines, parsley, potatoes, radish, spinach, strawberries, sweet pepper and turnips. Do not plant peas with onions or garlic.

PEPPERMINT

Peppermint repels white cabbage moths, aphids and flea beetles. As with all kinds of mint it is the menthol content that acts as an insect repellent. Bees and other beneficial insects love the flowers.

PEPPERS

Plant them near parsley, basil, tomatoes, geraniums, marjoram, lovage, petunia and carrots. Onions also make excellent companion plants for peppers, but don't plant them near fennel or kohlrabi.

PENNYROYAL

Repels fleas, mosquitoes and gnats. With a spreading habit, it can be used as a useful low-growing ground cover.

PETUNIA

These repel the asparagus beetle, leafhoppers, aphids and general garden pests. A good companion to tomatoes, but they can be planted just about anywhere. The leaves can be used in a tea to make a potent insect spray.

POACHED EGG PLANT
(Limnanthes douglasii)

Grow poached egg plants with tomatoes as they will attract hoverflies which eat aphids. Sprinkle the tiny seed in clumps wherever you want the plants to grow. They are annuals and so are very fast growing.

POTATOES

Companions for potatoes are bush beans, members of the brassica family, carrots, parsnips, celery, sweetcorn, dead nettles, flax, horseradish, marigolds, peas, petunia, onions and tagetes marigolds. Protect them from scab by putting comfrey leaves in the trench with your potato tubers at planting time. This also provides a nutrient rich feed for the potato plants as they develop – just like digging in animal manure. Horseradish planted at the corners of the potato patch provides general protection. Don't plant the following around potatoes: asparagus, cucumber, kohlrabi, parsnips, members of the squash family, sunflower, turnips and fennel. Keep potatoes and tomatoes apart too as they are both susceptible to blight and can infect each other.

PUMPKIN

Good pumpkin companions are sweetcorn, melon and other squashes. Plant a few marigolds (tagetes) in the vicinity to deter beetles. Nasturtiums will also act as an insect / pest repellent. Oregano / wild marjoram will also provide general pest protection.

PUSLANE

This edible weed makes good ground cover all around the garden, but pull it up before it goes to seed otherwise it will become a nuisance rather than a helper in the garden. You can use it raw in salads, lightly boiled or in stir-fries.

RADISH

Who would have thought that the little radish could play such a versatile and useful role in companion planting? Remember that they are part of the brassica family and this needs to be borne in mind when planning your crop rotations. Companions for radishes are leaf beet, beetroot, bush beans, climbing beans, carrots, chervil, cucumber, lettuce, melons, nasturtiums, parsnips, peas, spinach and members of the squash family. Radishes are a deterrent against cucumber beetles and chervil and nasturtium will improve the radishes' growth and flavour. Radishes are a favourite food of flea beetles so can be used as a sacrificial crop in the brassica bed. Plant these at 6 to 12 inch intervals amongst broccoli. In one trial this measurably reduced damage to the broccoli. Radishes will also lure leaf miners away from spinach. The damage the leaf miners do to radish leaves does not stop the radish roots from growing, so you will still be able to harvest a decent radish crop. Keep them away from hyssop plants.

RASPBERRY

A planting of garlic close to raspberry canes will discourage many flying pests. Keep the surrounding area free from weeds by using a thick layer of mulch. This will also help moisture retention – essential, especially when the fruits are developing.

RHUBARB

This is a good companion for all brassicas. Try planting cabbage and broccoli plants in your rhubarb patch and both of them will benefit from each other's company. Rhubarb will also protect beans against blackfly. Other good companions are garlic, onions and roses. A spray made from boiled rhubarb leaves containing the poison oxalic acid may be used to prevent blackspot and aphid attack on roses. In the flower garden rhubarb will protect columbines (aquilegia) from attack from red spider. Uncooked rhubarb is poisonous if eaten, but the large leaves make a good addition to the compost heap.

ROSEMARY

A useful, hardy perennial culinary herb and an excellent companion plant to cabbage, beans, carrots and sage. A very strong smelling scent deters cabbage moths, bean beetles and carrot root flies. Scatter a few cuttings around the growing tops of carrots to prevent attack from carrot flies.

RUE

An effective deterrent for aphids, flea beetle, onion maggots, slugs, snails, flies and beetles in roses and raspberries. Companions for rue are roses, fruits (in particular figs), raspberries and lavender. To make it even more effective against pests, crush a few leaves to release the smell before scattering them around your plants. You should not plant it near cucumber, cabbage, basil or sage. A pretty perennial with bluish-gray leaves, but go carefully when touching the plants as the sap can cause skin irritation.

Chives grown around your roses will help prevent blackspot and garlic repels aphids. Rhubarb too is a good partner for roses, even though unconventional; it provides soil protection and ground cover to suppress weeds. See under the rhubarb entry regarding a spray made from rhubarb. The small shrubby herb santolina also makes a good growing companion for roses as its scent repels pests and provides a source of ground cover.

SAGE

Use this pungent perennial herb as a companion plant with broccoli, cauliflower, rosemary, cabbage, and carrots to deter cabbage moths, flea beetles and carrot flies. Don't plant it near cucumber, onions or rue. Allowing sage to flower will also attract many beneficial insects into your garden as well as introducing a welcome splash of colour. Look out for varieties of sage with variegated foliage that can be used for their ornamental as well as practical qualities ('tricolour',. 'Icterina').

SANTOLINA
(Cotton Lavender)

Tolerant of dry conditions and poor soil, this silvery shrub is a natural insect repellent and several plants can be grown into a low growing hedge. The round yellow flowers are attractive to many beneficial insects like hoverflies and bees.

SAVORY SUMMER AND WINTER

Summer and winter savory are two of the most aromatic and easy to grow Mediterranean herbs and should be in everyone's garden. Both have hints of thyme and oregano with just a little pepperiness. Historically these two plants were grown near bee hives, providing nectar for honey production. Both plants have small pale purple flowers which the bees love. They are also great companion plants because their essential oils help mask the scent of other plants, making it hard for pests to find their targets.

SWISS CHARD LEAF BEET

This is a good plant for adding minerals to the soil. Rich in magnesium, the old leaves are perfect for adding to the compost heap once they are too tough to eat. They are beneficial to beans, with the exception of runner beans which will restrict their growth. Other companions for leaf beet are lettuce, onions and all the brassicas. Other helpful plants are garlic and mints. These are said to improve both growth and flavour.

SPINACH

Plant your annual spinach with peas and beans as these plants will provide natural shade for the spinach, preventing leaf scorch and soil dryness. Moist soil will help your spinach crop last longer before running to seed. Good companions for spinach are cabbage, cauliflower, celery, aubergines, onions, peas, and strawberries.

SQUASHES
(marrows, courgettes, pumpkins)

Good companions for any members of the squash family are sweetcorn and cucumber, and of course they will grow happily with others of their own kind. A few borage plants grown nearby will improve their growth and flavour. Marigolds will deter squash enemies such as bugs and beetles, as do nasturtiums and oregano.

STRAWBERRY

Friends of strawberries are beans, borage, lettuce, onions, spinach and thyme. The enemies are cabbage, broccoli, Brussels sprouts, cauliflower and kohlrabi. Borage will strengthen resistance to insects and disease. Never plant strawberries where tomatoes, potatoes, peppers or aubergines have been previously grown in the past four years. These crops can carry the root rot fungus verticillium which can also attack strawberries.

SWEETCORN

Sweetcorn is a very social plant with a wide range of ideal companions including amaranth, beans, cucumber, white geranium, melons, morning glory, parsley, peas, potatoes, pumpkin, squash and sunflowers. A classic example is to grow climbing beans up corn while inter-planting pumpkins. The sweetcorn provides a natural climbing frame for the beans (or morning glory), pumpkins smother the weeds and help the sweetcorn roots to retain moisture. Sweetcorn is a heavy feeder and the beans fix nitrogen from the air into the soil. The beans won't nourish the corn while it is growing, but when the bean plants die back they return nitrogen to the soil. Growing a deep rooting green manure such as ryegrass or mustard to follow sweetcorn will draw up nutrients from the subsoil to where the next crop can reach them.

SUNFLOWERS

Sunflowers give a big boost to sweetcorn, and are also attractive to ants which move aphids onto them, thus keeping the pests away from neighbouring plants. Grow a few of them close to aphid-prone plants and you will see first-hand the ants at work. Amazing!

SWEET ALYSSUM

Sow direct or set out young plant of sweet alyssum near plants that have been attacked by aphids in the past. Alyssum flowers attract hoverflies whose larvae devour aphids. Another plus is that their blooms draw bees to pollinate early blooming fruit trees. They will reseed freely and make a beautiful ground cover every year.

TANSY

Plant tansy with fruit trees, roses and raspberries, keeping in mind that it can become invasive. It also benefits cabbages and grapevines. As it contains a high potassium content, tansy will improve the growth of surrounding plants and because of this it makes it a useful ingredient to add to the compost heap. The strong scented leaves and yellow flowers also make it useful as an insect repellent - tansy cuttings sprinkled around will help keep ants away. The scent also deters many flying insects, fleas, beetles and rodents. A bunch of dried tansy can be hung up and used as a fly repellent in the house. Bear in mind that tansy is poisonous if eaten.

TARRAGON

Plant this throughout the garden as it is a great pest repellent. Recommended to enhance the growth and flavour of other vegetables.

THYME

Creeping varieties of thyme make a very useful ground cover. Look out for creeping red, creeping lemon or woolley thyme which will spread in a relatively short space of time. Thyme is easy to grow from either seeds or propagated from cuttings. The small flowers may not smell very attractive to us, but to bees they are heaven and they will fly in from near and far to feast on them.

TOMATOES

Tomato allies are many and varied: asparagus, basil, beans, carrots, celery, chives, cucumber, garlic, head lettuce, marigolds, mint, nasturtiums, onions, parsley, peppers, pot marigold and sow thistle. One drawback with tomatoes and carrots is that tomato plants can stunt the growth of your carrots, although they will still have good flavour. Basil will repel whiteflies, as does the ever useful marigold. Borage, lemon balm, chives and mint will improve the health and flavour of both the plants and fruit. Young dill plants improve the tomatoes' growth and health, but once mature, dill will start to have a detrimental effect. One enemy is kohlrabi which will stunt tomato growth. Also keep potatoes and tomatoes apart as they are both susceptible to blight and will contaminate each other. Fennel and rosemary are bad companions too and don't plant tomatoes under walnut trees as they may be affected by walnut wilt – very few plants thrive close to walnuts anyway.

TURNIPS

These root vegetables are undemanding and fast growing and all parts of the plant are edible, both roots and leaves. A member of the brassica family, the main enemy of turnips is club root which can be avoided by annual crop rotation. Good friends for turnips are catmint, peas, radish and thyme.

WORMWOOD

Wormwood will keep animals out of the garden when planted as a border and is an excellent deterrent to most insects. Don't plant it with peas or beans. A tea made from it will repel cabbage moths, slugs, snails, black flea beetles and fleas effectively.

YARROW

Yarrow has insect repelling qualities and makes an excellent natural fertilizer as it is high in copper. It is a good activator for the compost heap. The bright yellow flowers attract predatory wasps and ladybirds as well as many other beneficial insects in the summer. Yarrow will increase the vigour of its neighbouring plants and boosts the essential oil content of herbs when planted close to them.

A QUICK GUIDE TO COMMON PESTS AND DISEASES AND THEIR COMPANION PLANT SOLUTIONS		
Pest/Disease	**Affects**	**Solution**
Ants	Anywhere	Tansy, mint, pennyroyal, southernwood
Aphids	Tomatoes, beans, lettuce	Basil, marigold, catnep, chervil, garlic, rue
Apple scab	Apple trees	Chives
Asparagus beetle	Asparagus	Tomatoes, petunia
Bean beetle	Legumes (beans, peas)	Rosemary
Blackspot	Roses	Chives
Cabbage white butterfly	Brassicas	Thyme, rosemary, mint, sage, chamomile, nasturtiums
Carrot root fly	Carrots, parsnips	Onion family, sage, rue, rosemary, wormwood
Codling moth	Apple trees	Nasturtiums, garlic
Cumcumber beetle	Cucumber, melon	Radish, oregano
Flea beetle	Brassicas	Radish (as a sacrificial crop)
Fleas	Anywhere	Tansy, mint
Fruit fly	All fruit	Basil, garlic, onions, tansy
Mice	Anywhere	Southernwood, wormwood, catmint, catnep
Moths	Anywhere	Lavender
Powder/downy mildew	Cucumber, gooseberry	Chives
Slugs/snails	Delicate leaved crops and all young seedlings	Comfrey, chervil, rue, leeks, catnep, southernwood
Squash beetles	Courgettes, marrow, squash, pumpkin	Marigold
Thrips	Onions	Basil
Whitefly	Tomatoes, cucumber, brassicas	Marigold, nasturtium, basil

INSECT HOST PLANTS	
Many beneficial insect predators of plant pests can be attracted into the garden by including some of their favourite plants.	
Plant	**Insect**
Armaranth	Ground beetle
Aster	Butterflies, hoverflies
Borage	Bees
Buckwheat	Hoverflies
Caraway	Bees, beneficial wasps
Celery (flowers)	Beneficial wasps
Chamomile	Hoverflies, beneficial wasps
Chervil	Hoverflies, beneficial wasps and others
Clover	Bees, hoverflies, beneficial wasps
Coriander (flowers)	Bees
Dandelion	Bees, hoverflies
Dill	Hoverflies, beneficial wasps
Fennel	Hoverflies, beneficial wasps
Golden rod	Hoverflies
Hyssop	Bees
Lavender	Most nectar loving insects
Ivy	Hoverflies and beneficial wasps
Marigold	Hoverflies
Mint	Hoverflies, beneficial wasps, earthworms
Nettles	Bees, butterflies, many beneficial insects
Parsley (flowers)	Beneficial wasps and hoverflies
Poached egg plant	Hoverflies
Savory	Bees
Sunflower	Lacewings, beneficial wasps
Sweet Alyssum	Bees, hoverflies
Tansy	Ladybirds
Yarrow	Predatory wasps, ladybirds, many beneficial insects

COMPANION PLANTING TABLE FOR POPULAR FRUIT & VEGETABLES

Plant name	Helped by	Companions	Attracts	Enemies	Comments
Apple	Other apple trees of same pollination group	Chives, foxgloves, garlic, onions, sweet woodruff, wallflowers, nasturtiums	Pollinating insects	Potatoes	Do not allow surrounding grass in orchards to encroach on young, newly planted trees. Always keep trimmed in any case
Apricot		Basil, garlic, onions, tansy, asparagus, strawberries	Pollinating insects when in flower		Provide a shelter belt to protect tree from strong winds and extreme weather
Asparagus		Tomatoes, dill, coriander, comfrey, parsley, marigolds		Onions, garlic, potatoes	Keep asparagus beds weed-free at all times. Weeds will impede the growth of spears. Tomatoes protect asparagus against asparagus beetles
Aubergine	Beans, peppers	Amaranth, beans, peas, spinach, tarragon, thyme and marigolds		Fennel	Member of the nightshade family so also grow with potatoes and tomatoes. Marigolds repel nematodes
Beet	Lettuce, kohlrabi, onions and brassicas	Kohlrabi, onions, dwarf beans, lettuce, brassicas, other leaf beets		Runner beans and other tall plants	Leaves are particularly rich in minerals so good for composting. Runner beans and beets stunt each others' growth; any tall plants cast too much shade
Brassicas		Geraniums, dill, rosemary, nasturtiums, borage, onions, garlic and chives		Mustards, tomatoes, peppers	Plant nasturtiums as a trap plant for aphids. Strong smelling herbs deter whitefly
Carrots	Tomatoes, all alliums, lettuce	Alliums, rosemary, wormwood, sage, beans, flax	Lacewings, predatory wasps and other beneficial insects	Dill, parsnip, cow parsley	Tomatoes benefit from growing with carrots, but may stunt the carrots' growth. Beans provide nitrogen. Aromatic companion plants repel carrot fly. Interplanted onions and carrots confuse onion and carrot flies.
Celery	Leeks	Leeks, beans, dill, cosmos, snapdragons			
Sweetcorn	Beans	Amaranth, beans, cucumber, white geranium, melons, morning glory, parsley, peas, potatoes, pumpkin, squash, sunflowers		Tomatoes, celery	A principal plant in the three sisters planting scheme. A perfect tall plant to use to support others, eg climbing beans.
Cucumber		Nasturtiums, radishes, marigolds, sunflowers, peas, beets, carrots, dill	Beneficial for ground beetles	Rue, sage	Plant alongside sweetcorn or sunflowers and allow to climb
Leek	Celery, apple trees	Apple trees, carrots, celery and onions		Legumes	Same likes and dislikes as other members of allium family

Lettuce		Beets, bush beans, climbing beans, cabbage, carrots, cucumber, onions, radish and strawberries		Celery, cabbage, cress, parsley	Strong smelling herbs such as sage and mint repel slugs and snails.
Onion family (alliums)	Fruit trees, tomatoes, peppers, potatoes, brassicas, carrots	Carrots, leeks, leaf beet, kohlrabi, strawberries, brassicas, dill, lettuce and tomatoes		Peas, asparagus	Alliums include onions, garlic, leeks, shallots, chives and others and all share the same companion likes/dislikes
Potatoes		Bush beans, brassicas, carrots, parnips, celery, sweetcorn, dead nettles, lax, horseradish, marigolds, peas, petunias, onions, tagetes		Asparagus, cucumber, kohlrabi, parsnips, squash, sunflowers, turnips, fennel	Place comfrey leaves in potato trenches when palnting (prevents scab and provides nutrients). Horseradish grown nearby increases the disease resistance of potatoes
Pumpkins, squash	Sweetcorn, beans	Sweetcorn, melon, squash, marigolds, nasturtiums	Spiders, ground beetles		Flea beetles and other pests are deterred by marigolds and nasturtiums. Squash can be used in the three sisters planting system.
Spinach		Cabbage, cauliflower, celery, aubergine, onions, peas and strawberries			Keep soil around spinach moist to prevent bolting. Interplanting with peas or beans will help keep them shaded and stop them drying out
Tomatoes	Asparagus	Asparagus, basil, beans, carrots, celery, chives, cucumber, garlic, lettuce, marigolds, mint, nasturtiums, onions, parsley, peppers, sow thistle		Sweetcorn, fennel, peas, dill, potatoes, beetroot, kohlrabi, cabbage, cauliflower, rosemary, walnut	Tomatoes and potatoes are related so both are susceptible to blight. Growing them apart stops cross-contamination
Peppers	Basil	Onions, basil, tomatoes, geranium			General requirement of peppers very similar to basil, so grow them together
Radish	Brassicas - use radish as a sacrificial crop to attract flea beetles	Leaf beet, beetroot, bush beans, turnips, climbing beans, carrots, chervil, cucumber, lettuce, melons, nasturtiums, parsnips, peas, spinach, squash			Radish will also deter cucumber beetles and spinach leaf miners
Turnips		Catmint, peas, radish, thyme			Member of brassica family

INDEX

The Good Life Press Ltd.
The Old Pigsties
Clifton Fields
Lytham Road
Preston PR4 0XG